This book belongs to

Tuck

Ann R. Thomas.

From Paddock to Saddle

From Paddock to Saddle

Captain Elwyn Hartley Edwards

Nelson

Thomas Nelson and Sons Ltd
36 Park Street London W1Y 4DE

PO Box 18123 Nairobi Kenya

Thomas Nelson (Australia) Ltd
171–175 Bank Street South Melbourne Victoria 3205 Australia

Thomas Nelson and Sons (Canada) Ltd
81 Curlew Drive Don Mills Ontario

Thomas Nelson (Nigeria) Ltd
PO Box 336 Apapa Lagos

© E. Hartley Edwards 1972

First published 1972
Reprinted 1973

0 17 147222 5

Printed in Great Britain by
Butler & Tanner Ltd, Frome and London

Contents

Introduction

In this book I have attempted to present in two defined sections a logical progression of training for the young horse. For the sake of clarity, both are divided into phases, and, as I have been at pains to point out, each phase in the progression must necessarily overlap its neighbours.

The first section, devoted to the training of the three-year-old, can be considered as a sort of equine kindergarten, through which the horse progresses up to the level of the first class in the primary school. In the following section, carried out when the horse is in his fourth year, the primary education is completed and the horse goes on to acquire what may be likened to a secondary education. From this point the horse is then prepared – should his owner wish it – to receive higher education in whatever specialist field he seems best suited, whether it be dressage, show-jumping, eventing or even point-to-pointing.

The majority of riders, particularly those whose time is limited, will probably not wish to go further than the secondary stage, were it indeed within their compass, and, in truth, there will not be many horses able to do so, since these sports, at their higher levels, demand conformation and specific talents denied to all but a few. Nevertheless, and it is perhaps not sufficiently realized, a sound basic education, at least up to a secondary level, is as necessary to a horse as it is to a child if either are to fulfil a useful function in adult life.

This sort of training, in the third and fourth years of the animal's life, if carried out carefully and with commonsense, should produce a strong reliable and obedient all-rounder, able to give his owner a good day's hunting, be a calm hack, whose balance and paces make riding a pleasure, and be sufficiently proficient to take part in competitive sports at a good local level. In fact, the sort of horse we are all looking for. Perhaps even more importantly, good early schooling, designed in the first instance to build up muscles gradually and then to develop them in the correct supple form, will result in a sound horse having a far greater expectancy of a useful, working life.

Unfortunately, as the popularity of riding increases and

more people aspire to horse-ownership, the number of badly-trained or virtually untrained horses grows in corresponding measure – it's a sort of equine Parkinson's Law. In part, this comes about because although there is a greater awareness of the importance of training, the rapid extension of riding and horse-ownership has far outstripped the supply of competent instructors and skilled trainers. There are, of course, as a glance at any local newspaper will show, quite a lot of persons who advertise that they are able to take horses to 'break', a word which I have deliberately avoided throughout the text, as I prefer to think of 'making' a horse rather than of 'breaking' him. But, if one is to judge by the quantities of peculiarly-shaped animals to be seen from Land's End to John O' Groats, all exhibiting – since their very shape prohibits them from doing anything else – every form of equine problem, the word 'break', as used in most advertisements, is particularly appropriate. In fairness it may be that some of these animals were backed and schooled correctly enough and were then spoilt by a rider who had not had the same educational advantages, but it is more probable that whilst this factor is contributory to the disobediences and deficiencies in the horse, their root is in the animal's insufficient basic training. With some possible exceptions, we can therefore attribute the resistances and evasions we find in so many horses to human inadequacy. What is certain is that they are rarely the fault of the horse.

In writing this book I have sought to highlight the essentials in training and have stressed continually the necessity of preparing the horse, both physically and mentally, for each stage in the progression so that the trainer is always working well within the capacity of his horse at any time. I do not claim that anyone following this progression, and employing the methods advocated, will not have difficulties over and above those mentioned, since horses are essentially individuals, and it would be rare for any two to react in exactly the same way. Nonetheless, I would hope that somewhere in the book the amateur trainer could find at least an indication of how the problem would be best approached.

Essentially, this is a book for the rider who, having become increasingly dissatisfied with a number of horses at sixth and seventh hand, decides upon trying to do the whole job for himself. I would not want it to persuade a complete beginner into thinking that with this volume in one hand and a lunge whip in the other he is competent to undertake the making of a youngster. He would be far better advised, for a start, to read the book, or one like it, and then to learn the techniques required under some experienced person. I felt so strongly on this point that I included a very short chapter on the qualities required of a trainer, and elsewhere I have given great emphasis to his aids, and the manner in which they should be applied when he is teaching them to the young horse. If I have been guilty of over-emphasis, it was because I wanted to make it clear that the success of the exercise depends upon the trainer having taken the trouble to acquire a sound foundation of knowledge and practice himself before trying to impart the rudiments of an education to his horse. It is not possible to teach beyond the limit of your own knowledge and, in fact, it is unwise to go even that far. It is much better to teach to a standard one stage lower than your own level of competence.

Similarly, let me warn those who want to produce trained horses in double-quick time that this is not the book for them. It may be possible to shorten the suggested training programme but, of the short-cuts I know, only a few are effective, and then in nothing less than the most expert hands. Many more only lead to the establishment of serious and often ineradicable faults. Those that hope to find fascinating expositions on the use of 'gadgets' will be just as disappointed. It is true that I have included chapters on the more advanced methods of lungeing, but these cannot be regarded as approaching the insidious realms of the gadget. They are, after all, accepted practices among horsemen who would set their faces against the dumb jockey and the 'bending' tackle, and would regard the over-application of the whip as being in the province of the incompetent. What is more important is that there are good and logical reasons to support the use of these possibly unfamiliar lungeing methods. On the other hand, anyone who doubts his or her ability to put them to effective use would be well advised to leave them alone.

It is, in fact, a case of taking my own advice, in this respect, that has resulted in the chapter on long reins being devoted, largely, to an argument against their use. I admit, that the long reins *can* serve a useful purpose and that they do so in a small number of very skilled hands. I confess, however, that I am not very adroit in their management, and as I believe it possible to achieve all that is required without them in the stages of the training described in this book, I have not examined long-reining in any detail.

Although *From Paddock to Saddle* is concerned, primarily, with the training of the young horse much of the work discussed is just as applicable to the re-training of the older, spoilt horse, since it is only by returning to fundamentals, correcting the previous omissions in these stages, that an improvement will be made.

We hear a lot these days, and quite properly, about the rights of the young to receive the best education that it is possible to provide. I believe that our horses have a similar right to at least a basic education if we are to expect them to perform creditably in the varied fields that are open to us.

I am indebted to my friends, Christine Bousfield, for her drawings which accompany the text; Jennifer Baker, for her assistance in collating and typing my manuscript, and to Leslie Lane, for his advice and help with the photographs.

Dedham, 1972   E.H.E.

Part One

Chapter 1

The Anatomy of a Young Horse

One of the most common errors in training is the failure to recognize, and, therefore, to produce, the correct outline or 'form' in the young horse before ever contemplating mounted work.

At the outset let us be quite clear what is meant by a horse in the correct form, for it is a term that will be used continually. Form means shape, and in the early stages our efforts are largely directed to this end. We require a rounded top-line on the young horse which will be accompanied by a lowered head and neck and hindlegs engaged beneath the body, so that they provide the full propulsive thrust of which they are capable. In this position the horse is best equipped to carry weight and we are able to develop his paces, balance, movements and, ultimately, his head carriage. To obtain this form involves the building up of muscle by exercises, strapping, etc., and then developing them correctly by the same means. Until this is effected the imposition of weight will only build up muscles in resistance or opposition to the burden that they are, as yet, unable to carry with ease. The back hollows, the hindlegs trail behind (thereby reducing their effectiveness by about fifty per cent or more), and we are likely to get a head and neck hollowed in front of the withers, with the nose carried in the air and evading the bit action. In fact, a wholly inefficient piece of equine machinery has been produced which will make it impossible for us to carry out even the simplest of movements with any degree of rectitude or effectiveness. What is more, by working a horse in this shape we are putting undue strain upon the structural parts and encouraging unsoundness.

There is a school of thought which holds that the backing process (the introduction of saddle and rider) is best carried out very early in the training, whilst the horse is yet undeveloped and consequently unable to make more than a token objection. It may, indeed, be easier, although I would hold that if the preparation for backing was sufficiently thorough it is unlikely to cause any trouble. But, in essence, what a fallacious argument this is. In order to avoid a little difficulty, which in any case need never arise, the success of all the subsequent training is put at risk. How stupid can you

1 An example of a horse in the 'wrong' shape. The tissue wrapped round the girth is to combat girth galls caused by the saddle sliding forward. Later, when the horse's carriage was corrected no more trouble was experienced with galling

2 The same horse after reschooling

get? For surely it is the very height of folly to spend six to eight months solid work in order to produce a useless animal which you ruined in the first few weeks.

It may not be essential for the trainer to be an expert in anatomy, but in my view he should have an overall understanding of the physical structure, and be able to relate it to the training progression well before he begins work on a young horse. Unless he has this knowledge he cannot really know what he is trying to achieve, nor will he be able to see and correct the faults in carriage and outline which are bound to occur.

I really believe, for instance, that whilst a lot of people talk about 'developing muscle' they have very little idea of why they should seek to develop it or of what part the muscles play. Still less do they appreciate how muscle should be developed. We still hear horsey folk talking about turning fat into muscle, completely ignoring the fact that the two are entirely different substances. You can remove surplus fat and develop muscle in its place but you can't effect a physical change of fat into muscle any more than you can change hair or hoof into that substance.

By reminding ourselves of the structure's composition, and by studying, however briefly, the functions of the principal components, we can begin to see how our training should progress, and just how many pitfalls exist when we start to work an immature youngster.

To start at the beginning; the skeleton of the horse, or of any other animal, is made up of *bones*. Where two bones meet, a *joint* is formed, and whilst this is a remarkable feat of engineering on the part of the Almighty, it remains the weakest part of the structure. The ends of the two bones making a joint are of a greater density than is found elsewhere in the bones, and as an additional preventative against wear on their surfaces they are separated by layers of gristle, known as *cartilage*. The whole is held together by *ligaments*, which, apart from joining bone to bone, serve the purpose of limiting the extension of the joint, permitting it to move only as far as it is capable. *Any damage to a ligament will therefore affect the efficiency of the joint to which it is connected and cause trouble in the way of lameness.*

ligaments
groups of muscles

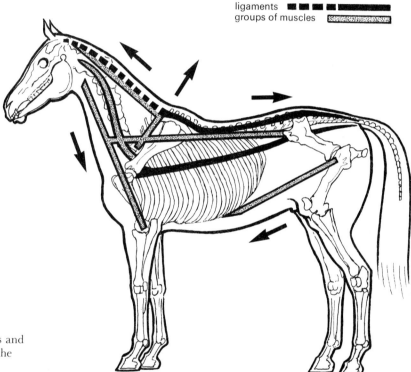

Figure 1
The principal groups of muscles and ligaments. The arrows indicate the direction of the exerted tension.

Now let us consider *muscle*, which is the substance covering the skeletal frame. By being attached to joints, muscle causes movement in these joints and therefore in the whole frame. Although muscle is possessed of great elasticity, it cannot, on its own, activate the joints, and produce the consequent loco-motion of the animal, without becoming torn and strained. Muscles are, therefore, equipped with *tendons* to help them in their job and to ensure that they do not sustain damage. A tendon is a sort of tough, inelastic rope connecting muscle

15

with bone. It is almost plaited into the substance of the muscle at one end and attached very firmly to the actual bone at the other. When the muscle contracts or extends the joint is then activated by the tendon moving in response to the contraction or extension of the connected muscle. *Should the tendon become sprained or otherwise damaged, it follows that the action of the joint must be more or less seriously impaired, dependent upon the extent of the injury.*

I have mentioned the elasticity of muscle and its ability to contract, thereby producing movement in the limbs. A peculiar property of contraction, however, is that the more a muscle is stretched the greater will be its capacity to contract. It must follow that the greater the capacity to contract in any one muscle, or group of muscles, the greater will be the degree of flexion possible in the joint or joints they activate, and the nearer will be their movement towards maximum efficiency. Since, however, muscles can only contract to the extent to which they can be extended, our object in training must first be to stretch the muscles of the young horse before we can expect him to produce any recognizable level of performance.

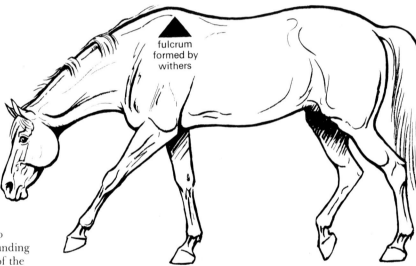

Figure 2
Encouraging a young horse to stretch the neck induces a rounding of the back and a stretching of the all-important cervical ligament running from the poll to the sacrum. The stretching effect is assisted by the ligament passing over the fulcrum formed by the withers.

A very important group of muscles to be considered in this stretching process are those running from the neck backwards on either side of the spine on the top line of the horse. These muscles are arranged in pairs on each side of what is known as the *ligamentum nuchae*, a very powerful elastic ligament extending from the poll to behind the withers, whence it continues, in a less elastic form and under an altered name, *ligamentum nucho-dorsale*, along the top of the spinal column to the sacrum at the croup of the horse. To avoid confusion let us refer to the whole of this ligament by the English term, the cervical ligament.

By inducing the horse to extend and lower his head and neck this ligament is stretched, but, more importantly, because it passes over the withers – which will then act as a fulcrum – the spine of the horse achieves a degree of tension and the back itself becomes arched or rounded. Whilst the back remains soft and slack and incapable of tension it is impossible for the horse to produce any pronounced propulsive effort. Further, if, whilst the horse has yet to develop and stretch the cervical ligament and its accompanying muscle structures, the rider is foolish enough to attempt to impose a carriage on his horse by raising the head forcibly, the result will be ruinous, since the back will be hollowed to an even greater extent, and it will be impossible for the hindlegs to propel the horse forward by being engaged well under the body. Now do you understand why you see so many poor wretched animals moving in a U shape, head in the air, back hollowed and hindlegs trailing in the next county?

This, however, is not quite the whole of the muscle story, since muscles can be said to be of two kinds, there are those that contract to flex a joint (flexors), and those that extend (extensors), which operate in opposite fashion. What is more, muscles, whilst frequently acting in pairs, can also act in opposition. In the instance of rounding the horse's back the large back muscles act as extensors, whilst to complete the rounding, raising the abdomen and bringing forward the hindlegs, three muscles on the sides of the abdomen and three running from the fifth and ninth ribs to the pubis act in opposition as flexors. Similarly, the tension of the muscles on the underside of the neck in the chest region are matched by an opposing tension of the dorsal muscles on the top of the neck. Between these opposite tensions, and as a result of them, the horse is able to carry his head and neck without conscious effort.

Examples of muscles acting in pairs, each compensating for the movement of its opposite number, are, again, the dorsal muscles on each side of the spine and those covering the stomach wall. These become compensatory when the horse bends his body, as he might do in making a turn. The muscles on the inside of the movement will then contract, whilst those on the outside must stretch correspondingly. *How important it is, therefore, if we are to be able to turn with equal ease to left or right, that these muscles should be of equal development and be able to stretch to the same degree.*

Why do horses turn more easily to the left than the right? Very simply, because the trainer, unwittingly, has encouraged the stretching and development of muscles on the right side of the horse and neglected those on the left. Consequently as

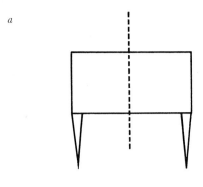

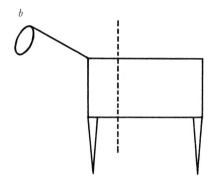

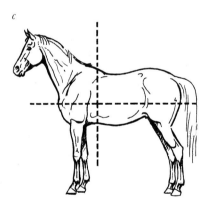

Figure 3
The point of balance in the horse. It is shown (*a*) in a rectangle, (*b*) in a rectangle with the addition of the balancing agents of head and neck causing the point to move forward, and (*c*) in the horse standing normally. Here the point has been fixed by intersecting the vertical line with a horizontal one drawn through the point of the shoulder.

the latter cannot stretch, the horse is unable to bend his body to the right. It just could be, of course, that the trainer has never given the matter a thought. In far too many cases a horse with this disability will be termed as 'one-sided in his mouth', and to correct this failing there will be recourse to peculiarly shaped bits, side-reins, ingenious arrangements of binder twine and so on. By the time these remedies have been put into action the horse really is 'one-sided' from nose to tail, and it is very unlikely that even the most gifted trainer will ever put him right again. Such are the dangers of acting on false premises.

To complete our understanding of the physical structure we have to know something about its balance, since this is a problem with which we shall be greatly concerned throughout our training programmes.

Although a great deal of talk goes on about balance, and even more is written about it, the implications of equilibrium, which are so essential in equitation, are not as thoroughly appreciated as they should be. If the horse were simply a rectangle supported on four pillars it would be obvious that the point around which the body would be balanced would be in the centre of the rectangle, in much the same way as the 'point of balance' (or the centre of gravity) of a child's see-saw is the central support which forms a pivot for the movement. The horse is not so far from being a rectangle, but because one end is made heavier by the addition of his head and neck his centre of gravity is moved forward correspondingly. Tests have shown that the centre of balance of the horse, when he is standing square (with head and neck held normally) is at the intersection of imaginary lines passing vertically from a point a little behind his withers through the centre of the body to the ground, and a second line drawn horizontally, and similarly through the body, from the point of the shoulder to the buttock.

This definition of the placement of the centre of equilibrium can be generally accepted as being correct, or nearly so, in most cases. The conformation of individuals, however, can alter the position of the centre. If, for example, we have a horse with a thick heavy neck and a great coffin of a head, more weight will be carried over the forehand and the point of balance will be shifted forward. At the other extreme, a horse with a short, thin neck and a tiny, blood-like head will carry less weight on the forehand and his centre will be positioned to the rear of the usually accepted point.

This point of balance, however, cannot be static, since it is bound to move in accordance with the movement of the horse and, most particularly, in accordance with the gestures made by the head and neck, which are the agencies by which the horse maintains his equilibrium, and which control the shift of the point of balance. The neck and the head can be likened to a pendulum with a weight on the end of it; if they are raised then more weight will be thrown on to the quarters and, as a result, the point of balance will move to the rear in accordance with the altered weight distribution. Conversely, if the head and neck are lowered more weight is put on the forehand and the centre of balance moves forward. Should the horse turn sharply, this shifting centre of balance must follow the movement and fall towards the inside of the turn.

The following figures, which are scientifically accurate and for which I am indebted to my friend, Professor Jean Froissard, illustrate very clearly the influence of the head and neck on the distribution of weight.

Taking a horse weighing 768 lb, standing squarely with the head held in a normal position, 420 lb of the total weight is carried on the forehand and 348 lb on the hindlegs, a difference of 72 lb. If the neck is lowered the weight on the forehand is increased to 536 lb and that on the quarters reduced to 232 lb, a difference of 304 lb. When the neck is raised, on the other hand, only 400 lb is placed over the forelegs and 368 lb is placed over the quarters, the difference being reduced to 32 lb. The point of these figures and of this dissertation on balance generally is to show how important is the freedom of head and neck, and also to reveal an objective in the later stages of training; that of working towards an improved balance under saddle, to be made by a natural raising of the head and neck which will entail a horse carrying more of his weight on his engaged hindlegs and so becoming lighter in front.

In addition, of course, the positioning of the horse's centre of gravity tells us just where our weight should be placed if we are not to interfere with his balance and inhibit the movement of his limbs. There is only one place for the rider's weight – it must be held as nearly as possible over the horse's centre of balance at all paces. Much later on, when the horse is developed and has reached a higher level of training we shall be discussing how the rider can impose a balance on the horse by the careful movement of his body weight, but for the moment let us go no further than this.

Incidentally, the effect of the rider sitting out of balance – too far in front or behind the horse's centre of balance – and the extent to which his weight has a bearing upon the total weight distribution can be gauged from the following figures. A rider weighing 128 lb, if he sits centrally and in accordance with the classical concept, places an additional 82 lb on the horse's forelegs and 46 lb on the hindlegs. If he employs a back-of-the-saddle seat inclining his body to the rear, 102 lb of his weight is carried on the hindlegs. How important it is then for the rider to learn to ride, and how essential that the trainer should take pains to develop the structure of his horse to the point where it is sufficiently strong to function to full advantage whilst carrying this extra burden.

In the light of what we have been discussing let us now consider the young horse we intend to train, and see how this knowledge can guide us in his early education.

If, once more, we think of the horse as a rectangular box with a leg at each corner we shall be forced to admit that the structure is not ideally designed for the carrying of weight, particularly as that weight is to be placed on the weakest part, the unsupported centre. And then his legs and feet (wonderful mechanisms though they are) are not really designed to withstand the excessive concussion incurred in trotting on hard roads, galloping, and, above all, jumping: at least, surely not when they are compelled to support a burden which may be as much as one-fifth of the horse's own weight, and which, by shifting about, will necessitate continual adjustments in the horse's own balance. By a careful process of physical training it is, however, possible to condition this seemingly ill-designed weight-carrier to carry a rider and also to teach him how to adjust his own balance for that purpose.

But make no mistake, the young, unridden horse, of, say, three years of age, is just not capable of carrying weight satisfactorily without damaging the various elements comprising his structure. For this very good reason the first stages of training are devoted to developing and strengthening his body and helping him to position and hold his body so that he can more easily carry his rider; something which we must achieve by, amongst other things, inducing tension in the spinal complex and a corresponding engagement of the hindlegs.

If we commence to ride him before he is physically ready, or we ride him for too long, his back, insufficiently muscled to bear weight, will naturally be hollowed in an effort to avoid the discomfort, and with it will come all the attendant ills associated with hollow backs – non-engagement of the hocks, minimal flexion of joints and a head carried in the air as a result of a 'caving-in' of the neck at the withers. As for improved balance, that doesn't enter into it at all. The horse is ruined before we have even started.

This leads us to a frequently asked question. At what age should a horse's training commence? In general it is accepted that a horse may start his primary school education at three years, after which he should be put out until the following year, when his secondary education can be begun. However, many authorities, amongst them Col. V. D. S. Williams (who has handled as many young horses as any man) will hold that it is better to leave the introduction to school until four and to commence the further education at five. I would agree with this course of action although I realize that many people, for economic reasons or otherwise, will take an opposite view.

What is absolutely certain is that the horse does not mature until about his sixth year. Until this time his bone structure is still relatively green and soft and therefore liable to become distorted by work. Moreover, the muscle structure, ligaments and tendons, as well as the internal organs are not fully developed and are therefore more easily subjected to strain. Just as importantly, since mental conditioning is of equal importance with physical development, no horse under three is able to concentrate sufficiently on the work expected of him. It is like expecting a six-year-old child to appreciate Einstein's Theory of Relativity.

It is, of course, possible to begin training and riding a horse well before he has reached three years but by doing so his useful working life is shortened appreciably. The risk of causing permanent and premature unsoundnesses by imposing weight on an immature frame are very real and there is also the danger of spoiling his temperament for good.

I am well aware that racehorses run as two-year-olds, but in view of the wastage involved and the number of unsound animals the practice produces (some of whom are so affected as to be unable to breed), this can hardly be considered as an argument in favour of working at an early age.

It might be asked that, if this is the case, why do we not wait until six, when the horse is fully grown, before backing him? Apart from it being beyond most people to keep a horse doing nothing for six years and bearing in mind the average life span of the equine, there are other good reasons, although they need not prevent you from tackling an un-made six-year-old if you happen to have one. In my experience a horse of this age has really developed almost too much. He is far less amenable to discipline after having run wild for six years and, whilst that may be overcome, he has also had time to become set in his physical development. Far more work will be required to obtain equal muscular development, if it is possible at this stage; in addition the natural slight curvature of the spine has had opportunity to become established.

This spinal curvature is something common to all equines in one degree or another, and is frequently accentuated in training rather than corrected. Why the spine should be other than straight is not entirely certain, but it is possibly caused by the foetal position of the unborn foal within the womb. Whatever the reason, the result of the curvature is to prevent the animal moving straight. By moving straight we mean that the hindfeet follow exactly the track of the forefeet. This is rarely the case in the young horse, whose hindlegs tend to make a track slightly out of alignment with that of the forefeet. Although the spine itself is for the larger part entirely rigid, a certain degree of flexibility is possible in the lumbar vertebrae and in the area of the sacrum. Much of our training exercises are aimed at correcting this natural crookedness by increasing and controlling the flexibility in these regions. The purpose of straightening the horse is to improve his mechanical efficiency by positioning the thrust of his hindlegs immediately behind his forehand, rather than to one side of it, when the maximum effect of the propulsive force would naturally be diminished and, therefore, less efficient in terms of simple mechanics.

A horse who starts his education at four years, or even at three, will, all else being equal and if his training is carried out intelligently, continue in useful work until he is twenty or more. I doubt very much if this would be the case with an animal backed at two, or earlier, and ridden in all sorts of activities thereafter.

The great lesson to be learnt and the one that we must always remember when we set out to train a young horse is that work must always be *within* his physical capacity at any given moment. It is all too easy to go too fast when we think the horse is beginning to go well. It is far more difficult to go slowly, but this is what we must do.

All resistances, all disobediences, have their roots in incorrect elementary training and they are frequently the result of overwork in the very early stages. Stiffness and soreness are easily caused in the muscles, joints, etc., of the young horse, and when they occur the horse is driven into disobedience to avoid further pain. If we persist, he feels he has been treated unjustly, and becomes resentful. Thereafter it becomes a battle between man and horse instead of a gradually ripening partnership. The same thing will happen if we ask too much of his limited mental process, a subject which we will deal with in the next chapter.

Chapter 2

The Nature of the Horse

In the preceding chapter we discussed the physical structure of the horse and emphasized the importance of preparing his body for work.

But the body and its development represents only fifty per cent of the trainer's job. To produce the 'whole' horse we must be just as concerned with the development of his mind and the encouragement of his powers of concentration. All too frequently, I suspect, we concentrate on physical performance without recognizing that performance is as much the result of mental attitudes as of physical ability. In any field – dressage, show-jumping or what you will – a good performance is, to a very great extent, a physical manifestation of a state of mind, and the trainer who ignores the mental aspects involved in schooling is unlikely to get very far with his pupil.

Elsewhere we have compared the education of the horse with that of the human child. But whilst we may do this in general terms there are specific differences, the greatest of these being that we are dealing with two distinct species. The human is characterized by his ability to reason, the animal, denied this capacity, is motivated almost entirely by instinct. To train horses, it is essential that we have a clear understanding of the way in which their very small minds work and appreciate how limited they are in this department.

Possibly the greatest mistake we can make is to attribute to the horse an intelligence which he does not possess. By doing so we run the risk of overtaxing his mental capacity, which is as much fraught with danger as that of putting too great a strain on his physical structure. In the last instance we may make the horse stiff and sore and so drive him into making defensive resistances, and much the same thing happens if we ask too much of his limited mental powers.

We have to recognize that the horse is not a human being and cannot, therefore, be expected to react in the same way as one. Nor should we think of him in the same terms as the dog. Again, there is a fundamental difference, for the good reason that whilst both are animals they belong to quite separate and distinct species, whose mental attitudes have been created by wholly unrelated environments. A dog, because of

3 A grand type of filly foal

his long and close association with man and by reason of his size, which allows him to be in constant contact with his master, sharing the home, the best armchair and in some cases having his place even in the bedroom, has developed a very close rapport between himself and his humans. How much of this rapport can be attributed to intelligence is, perhaps, debatable. It could be argued that his domestication has resulted in the formation of a great number of highly sensitive conditioned reflexes and that intelligence, by human definition, has nothing to do with the case. Be that as it may, our dogs remain the most constant beings we are likely to meet in our particular 'vale of tears'.

I remember many years ago (as a painfully earnest youth in the throes of a teenage religious fervour) discussing with my very unworldly aunt the relative roles of horses and dogs in the creation. She was a very gentle and patient elderly lady, by no means clever but possessed of an enviable simplicity, and I was a very volatile and importunate young man with a very good opinion of my intellectual capacity. To conclude what I now realize must have been a very trying discussion for her, my aunt said something that went roughly like this: 'If man,' she said 'was created in the image of God then, perhaps, the animals were created to show us the qualities of their Maker. Horses, to me, seem to be a symbol of majesty and power combined with great humility, whilst the dog must surely be the embodiment of everlasting love. And now it really is time I made the tea'. Home-spun philosophy, if you like, but she was quite right about the dog (and, perhaps, about the horse, too).

Is there any being, other than the dog, that gives complete and unquestioning devotion from the time as a wriggling pup he involuntarily wets the carpet in an ecstasy of affection until with a last feeble wag of his tail he passes out of our lives? After all, you can be the most unmitigated villain, steal your best friend's wife, abandon your children or murder your grandmother for the contents of her handbag, and to your dog you will still remain a god and the centre of his being. I don't know whether that is very intelligent behaviour, but I am prepared to accept it without question and with gratitude. But this book is not about dogs, but horses, and the point of my anecdotal digression is to emphasize the difference and to warn against confusing the one with the other.

There is no great harm done by implanting a smear of lipstick on a horse's muzzle as he is tucked up for the night if it induces a nice, warm feeling in the breast of the donor. But don't expect from the horse the same response as you might receive from your dog, or for that matter from a human recipient. Horses are singularly ill-equipped to express affection, which in any case they cannot do in recognizable human terms. They do not wag their tails, or at any rate when they do it means exactly the opposite of 'I do love you', and when they nuzzle you endearingly it is more likely that they are thinking of the titbit in your pocket than of anything else. This is not to say that we cannot win their trust and respect and establish a very satisfactory partnership with them – we can, but in order to do so we must understand what makes the horse tick and base our approach to him on that acquired knowledge. The extremes in the human approach to horses are what I would term as 'sentimental humanization' at one end and 'domination' at the other. Neither is desirable nor defensible since the horse is a creation in his own right, being neither child nor dog, nor still less an insensate brute. The characteristics and instincts which make up the often paradoxical personality of the horse are almost entirely derived from his early environment, and with the passage of the centuries they remain in him virtually unaltered.

In the beginning, the horse was a grass-eating herd animal and is still just that. He is no longer hunted by man for food (nowadays we are more civilized, some of us just herd him into terrifying continental markets to be left untended and without water until some twentieth-century cave-man delivers him from his suffering, in ways that are not much better than those employed by our skin-clad ancestors) nor is he preyed upon by carnivorous beasts – most of these are in zoos. But in the days of his freedom, before domestication, danger lurked behind every bush and stony outcrop and, not surprisingly, the horse developed a set of highly efficient defence mechanisms to ensure his survival.

Nature provided the horse with extraordinary powers of sight, hearing and smell, together with a highly developed *sixth* sense, and endowed him with the ability to move away at speed when attacked or when he suspected attack to be imminent. His existence in those early days was divided between a constant search for food and the avoidance of his enemies. These two factors, together with the reproductive urge at certain times of the year, were paramount in his life and still colour his outlook today, even though the conditions brought about by domestication are at such variance with those pertaining in the wild state.

We recognize that the horse's digestive system, for instance, has undergone no significant change over a period of many thousands of years, and that to keep him healthy it is a fundamental necessity for us to feed him in accordance with the requirements and limitations of his particular digestive apparatus. If the yew tree existed five thousand years ago and a horse was unwise enough to make a meal of its bitter foliage, he died pretty quickly. Similarly, should the twentieth-century horse fill his tummy with yew the result will be exactly the same.

What we must appreciate is that, just as the basic physical structure of the horse is much the same as it ever was, so are his inherited and deeply-rooted instincts. In the domestic state these instincts may be subdued, but it is just as impossible to eradicate them as it is to expect the horse to enjoy roast beef and two veg. for his Sunday lunch. At the grass roots of the horse personality are the primitive instincts combined with certain characteristics (brought into being by the domestic environment) and made complete by the senses (common to all creatures) and a memory as long and as accurate as that attributed to the elephant.

By examining the horse under these general headings the would-be trainer will obtain a deeper understanding of his pupil and a very good insight into the methods he should employ in his schooling. Let us look first at the instincts and characteristics, which for convenience I have subdivided into ten secondary headings, and then assess the effect of each one upon our training progression. Some we shall find can be used to our advantage, whilst others will act in the opposite fashion and will call heavily on our reserves of patience, tact and sympathy if their effect is to be reduced to an acceptable level.

These sub-divisions, which all tend to be interrelated to a

4 A well-made two-year-old who still has plenty of room for growth

certain degree, since we can rarely attribute a specific action on the part of the horse to any particular one, are as follows:

1 The Gregarious or Herd Instinct
2 A Sense of Security
3 The Following Instinct
4 Adherence to Routine
5 Laziness
6 Excitability
7 Nervousness
8 Innate Sensitivity
9 The Spirit of Co-operation
10 The Quality of Courage

5 A three-year-old who is a shining example of good early management

At first sight these appear to constitute a daunting and somewhat contradictory bunch, but then the horse is a creature of paradox.

Herd Instinct

The first of these, the **Herd Instinct**, is probably the strongest of all and exerts a corresponding influence on the horse's behaviour. It can, however, be overcome, at least in part, by training, and we can also make use of it in various ways.

As examples of the natural instinct being subjugated, by training, to the wishes of the rider we only have to think of the show-jumper, who leaves the collecting ring and the companionship of his own kind (temporarily, his herd) to enter the main arena and jump his round. Another instance would be that of the trained hunter jumping out of a lane crowded with horses to pursue an independent line of his rider's choice. In both cases, the training the horse has received enables him to respond in contradiction to the natural instinct. Conversely, the instinct to remain with, or return to, the herd can be exploited in the early schooling of the horse. A young horse acquires confidence, for instance, by being taken hunting, when he will jump obstacles in company that he would be chary of attempting in cold blood and, indeed, will frequently jump similar fences on his own in order to return to the other horses, should he have become separated from them. In fairness it should be recognized that another element is present in the hunting field which acts as a further encouraging factor. That is, excitement, brought about by the proximity of a fairly large number of horses; but more of that later. Using the herd instinct in much the same way we encourage the horse in his first jumping lessons by asking him to jump towards his stable and his companions. Most young horses will jump quite freely this way, whereas if we were to ask them to jump going in the opposite direction we might well be courting a refusal – something which we do not want to put in his mind at this or any other stage in his training. We will also find that when introducing some, but not all, of the movements on the flat for the first time we shall more easily obtain what we want if we face the horse towards the exit from the schooling area, when he will move with greater impulsion.

Racing is yet another example of exploiting the herd instinct, and, if we think about it, the argument that horses must love steeplechasing, because when one loses his jockey he continues to gallop and jump with the others, is not really a viable one. The horse, by keeping up with the others, is obeying the law of the herd, and I don't think for a moment that the question of enjoyment has any relevance at all. In fact, the deeper one probes into the nature of the horse the stronger becomes the conviction that the euphemisms employed by the racing journalists are really very wide of the mark.

Sense of Security

Complementary to the herd instinct is the **Sense of Security** which in the wild state is found in belonging to the herd. All species of life, or at any rate the more advanced ones, need to feel secure, and this is particularly applicable to the horse, a herd animal. Whilst we cannot attempt to simulate the true herd environment in the domestic horse it is, nevertheless, desirable to appreciate its importance and if at all possible to keep horses in company with their own kind. Horses kept singly frequently develop peculiar and often neurotic traits of behaviour which are rarely, if ever, noticeable where a number of horses live together, as in a riding school, racing stable or a military troop. I don't say that it is not possible to keep certain horses on their own but, like an only child, they will be more inclined to pose particular problems. Unlike the child, who has the advantage of being able to make friends of his own age at school and can have his chums round to tea during the holidays, the horse's isolation is much more complete. It is quite feasible for a dog to be content with human company in the absence of other dogs in the household, and I suppose it might be possible in the case of the horse, providing the human was able to share his stable and romp in the fields with him for each and every hour of the twenty-four which make up a day. But as this is unlikely to be practicable for even the most dedicated horse lover, a better solution would seem to lie in the provision of an equine companion, particularly in the case of the young horse.

In the human, security is centred in the home and, as we are continually told by all the psychologists, it is the home that has the greatest influence on the development of the child. Broken homes and unhappy ones, providing no firm base of security, tend to produce the majority of juvenile delinquents, whilst good homes and a happy family atmosphere are supposed to result in balanced personalities well equipped to make their contribution to the society in which they live.

For the horse, home, the centre of his security, is his box and immediate surroundings, and the atmosphere which is created in these places is just as important to him as that which exists for the human in his or her home. Its influence is a very strong one, largely, it should be recognized, because of its association with food – a matter of great preoccupation to the horse. Providing that the horse has not been subjected to punishment or ill-treatment in his stable which would cause him to relate it to unpleasant experiences he will always display great eagerness to return to it. Occasionally the almost irresistible attraction the box holds for the horse becomes a little too much of a good thing, and we must take care that it does not assume so great an importance as to frustrate our training. We should be asking for trouble, for instance, if our schooling area was sited very close to the stable. In such circumstances the nearness of the box, with its pleasant associations, would be uppermost in the horse's mind and we should find it difficult to obtain his concentration for the work of the moment.

On the other hand, the stable, and the return to it after work, is the greatest reward we can give to our horse, and there are a number of ways in which its appeal can be used as an aid in training. Invariably a horse perks up and goes better when returning home after exercise. His mind is then more occupied with thoughts of rest and food than with anything else that happens to be going on round him. Recognizing this fact, the wise trainer will always try to introduce his horse to road traffic by ensuring that he chooses a route where the heavier concentration will be encountered on the homeward leg. Very frequently a young horse will pass lorries, buses and the like quite happily within, as it were, the gravitational pull of the stable, when an hour earlier, on his outward journey, he would have made the strongest objections to their presence.

I think that everyone will recognize how essential is the sense of security to the horse if he is to be a calm and therefore a receptive individual, but I am not so sure that we understand how much time is needed before a horse relaxes and begins to feel secure in new surroundings.

Imagine what a traumatic experience it must be for a young three-year-old to be uprooted from the familiar surroundings of the stud at which he was born, transported half-way across the country to a frightening sale-yard and, finally, subjected to yet another bewildering journey before arriving at a new home. No wonder that he is wild-eyed, nervy and off his food for some days after what he has been through. Even older horses will react in this way at a change of stable. Indeed, it is not unusual when one acquires a new horse to find that for the first few days he may be reluctant to leave his box, in which he finds a tenuous security, and thereafter may nap in quite determined fashion in his attempts to return to it. Given time to become accustomed to his new home and his new owners, and treated patiently and kindly, he will regain his lost confidence and settle down, but if his new owner should make the mistake of punishing him he will only be adding to the confusion in the horse's mind and confirming the latter's feeling of insecurity.

The development of a strong sense of security in the pupil must be of paramount consideration in dealings with the young horse. Until it is attained and made firm we cannot think of beginning to teach the most elementary lessons.

The Following Instinct

Many of the natural instincts to be found in the horse, some of which are not entirely helpful from our viewpoint, can be subdued because of the horse's willingness to be led and his consequent dependence on a leader. By nature, horses are followers, they are not leaders, or, at least, that is true of the great majority. Members of a herd submitted happily (or were quickly put in their places if they didn't) to the dominant stallion, the herd leader upon whose sagacity and experience their safety and well-being depended.

Bereft, in the domestic state, of a herd stallion the need for leadership still remains. Fortunately, horses appear to be quite happy for a human leader to take the place of the stallion and can come to repose an astonishing degree of confidence, trust and reliance in the one who feeds them, cares for them and enforces a discipline over them.

There are, of course, those few horses who are not naturally followers and who in consequence demand very much more of a trainer if they are going to turn out satisfactorily. Most stallions come into this category and a few geldings who retain stallion characteristics, but never mares. In general such animals are better left alone by the beginner, although in the right hands they will be wonderfully rewarding subjects.

Adherence to Routine

The horse's love of routine is not instinctive but is a characteristic developed in, and as a result of, the domestic state. A settled, ordered routine of grooming, work and feeding contributes to a calm state of mind in the horse, who worries and gets himself agitated and excited if the routine is broken or something out of the ordinary occurs. Whilst it should be fairly easy to ensure that one's horse is fed at fixed and inviolable times, it is not always so simple, nor is it desirable, to avoid the unusual. A day at a show or an afternoon spent at an instructional rally or some such activity can be regarded as a break in the regular routine, but it would be quite unreasonable to forego these outings for that reason. Initially, they will cause a loss of calm, but our horses, like ourselves, have to learn to live in and with the world in which they find themselves. In addition, such excursions outside the immediate environment as well as broadening the experience act as an antidote to boredom, which is a far greater evil than a temporary loss of routine.

Laziness

I think that if an average group of horse owners were to be

asked whether they thought that horses enjoyed being ridden as much as their riders enjoyed riding them they would be somewhat nonplussed, since it is unlikely that they would have given any consideration to the matter. A great many of us, I am sure, assume that those activities which we regard as being commonplace and natural are regarded in the same light by our horses. The assumption disregards a fundamental truth about the horse. He is by nature a very lazy animal whose idea of heaven is an enormous field of lush grass in which he can graze undisturbed until his belly is full, and after a pleasant doze can start filling himself up all over again.

Work does not come naturally to the horse and why his owner should require him to gallop hither and thither and, above all, jump fences, some of which could be more easily walked round, must be entirely incomprehensible to him.

In his wild state the only time the horse galloped, except in play, was when the herd fled in panic from some attack; otherwise he moved slowly, browsing from one grazing ground to the next. Nor did the horse jump, for the very good reason that there was very little on his grazing grounds which made the exercise necessary, or certainly very little which could not be more easily circumvented by a slight change of direction. Jumping, indeed, is entirely unnatural to the horse and a natural jumper is therefore a very rare bird. It is true that some horses, by reason of their temperament or physique, are more fitted for jumping than others, but they all have to be taught. There is really no such thing as a natural jumper, and that is why no-one will ever succeed in establishing a stud to breed jumpers.

Carrying the argument a stage further, and into a different field, horses can hardly be said to race because they enjoy it. It seems more likely that a race is a pretty good simulation of the herd panic and that it is this, together with the high excitement engendered, that provides the necessary stimuli. Certainly the training of the racehorse although involving great expertise in his physical preparation and in the perception of his particular idiosyncrasies, is at a minimum in comparison with training in the context with which we are concerned.

Excitement

As we have touched so frequently on the word excitement, it is perhaps an appropriate place at which to examine this frequently frustrating element in the make-up of the horse.

Horses will become excited, and therefore inattentive, for almost any reason, many of them seeming to be quite illogical to the human mind – at least at first sight. A horse becomes excited when conditions are either reminiscent of his wild state or when he performs in a manner which is totally out-of-keeping to his nature.

Galloping excites horses, particularly in company, because it simulates the panic of the fleeing herd. And even when working on his own a young, untrained horse, and many older ones too, will tend to hot up the moment we start the work at canter. Jumping, an unnatural pursuit for the horse, has a similar effect. Indeed, in some cases, it produces the sort of result we might expect from a man who has imbibed too freely of the whisky bottle. The presence of other horses, or even of a single, strange horse in the near vicinity, is exciting. This is the herd instinct asserting itself again. Fear, too, will cause excitement, and it is surprising what seemingly trivial occurrences will arouse the innate instinct of self-preservation. Anything, from a rag in the hedge to the sudden appearance of a man with a wheelbarrow, or a woman pushing a pram, will be regarded with suspicion by the horse.

Obviously this tendency to excitement represents a considerable problem in training and it is one which is not always entirely overcome. What we can do, and it is a prime objective in the horse's education, is to keep excitement under control by teaching the horse obedience to our legs and hands so that he carries out potentially exciting work in a state of virtual calm. Calm, incidentally, is not synonymous with lethargy. Ideally, we are seeking a horse who performs with gaiety and even fire and yet retains a quietness of mind.

Previously I have referred to the exploitation of excitement as a contributory factor in the hunting field and in racing, but it can also be used, quite wrongly, in teaching, or in this case 'making', a horse to jump. Rough treatment of the horse by the rider – harsh use of the bit and unjustified punishment with whip and spur on the 'two in the guts and one in the mouth' principle – can induce a state of excitement from which a horse may be driven into jumping a fence out of desperation. But it is not to be recommended. It may work for a time under riders who are pleased to be known as 'strong' ('brutal' would be a better description) but in the end you produce a wildly neurotic creature with a pathological aversion to a 12-inch high cavalletto. Until that time comes the horse may jump after a fashion, but he will do so with the minimum of style, accuracy and safety and with a continual risk of straining his legs and back.

Nervousness

Essentially, the horse, despite his size and strength, is the most nervous and highly strung of creatures, which is natural enough when we consider that his survival mechanisms are based upon his ability to run away. Unlike the carnivores, he is not equipped to survive as an aggressor. He has teeth, certainly, but they are designed primarily to chew grass, and it is only in certain circumstances that they are used in an act of aggression. His legs too, are enormously powerful, but their purpose again is not entirely a belligerent one, even though they may be damaging on occasions. Their job is to carry their owner away from danger as fast as they can be laid to the ground. The horse's defence is always in flight. His reaction on seeing a strange object or, when startled, is to run away, not to attack. Consequently, he is prone to shy at strange objects, particularly if they move, or at sudden noises. Often a road-man's flag flapping in the hedge, or a plastic sack slung over a gate, will cause him to stop dead in his tracks and attempt to swing round and run off back along the way he come. Shying is, of course, annoying and can be dangerous, particularly on modern roads, and most young horses will go through a phase when they jump and start at all sorts of things, both real and imagined. They may, indeed, go so far as to give a buck or two, which in itself is part of the defensive mechanism. It is probable that the buck is an instinctive reaction made to dislodge an attacking animal, such as a mountain lion, which had leapt on to the victim's back in an attempt to bring him down. It is not, therefore, surprising that the horse should make use of this defence when startled, although the knowledge of its origin is hardly much comfort to the rider sitting on top. What is, perhaps, something to wonder at is that the horse, despite this association, should consent so easily to carrying us on his back at all.

Shying can, however, be reduced to a minimum if the rider acts quietly and with common sense – providing, that is, the horse is not suffering from defective vision.

The great thing to remember is that the horse should not be punished for shying, either deliberately, with whip or spur, or involuntarily by a jerk in the mouth caused by the rider's lack of security. Punishment in these instances only confirms the horse's fear and makes him even more nervous. What the frightened horse needs is to be given confidence by his rider's firm seat and soothing hand and voice. If possible, we should encourage the horse to approach the offending object, allowing him to smell and even touch it, whilst we continue to re-assure him.

Once there is complete trust between horse and rider, which is really what training is about, almost everything is possible, even with the most nervous of horses. My own mare is exceptionally highly strung yet is sufficiently obedient and has enough confidence in her rider to overcome her very natural fears. Not long ago I was riding down a narrow lane fronting a collection of miscellaneous caravans and trivia belonging to a gipsy family. They had lit a bonfire on the verge, in contravention of the law, on which had been piled a miscellaneous collection of rubbish including some cardboard boxes complete with packing straw. Had this frightening conflagration been confined to the verge it would have been hazard enough but it had been allowed to spread over the roadway, which was consequently blocked by a crackling mass of rubbish crowned with a heavy cloud of smoke. Through this my terrified mare, her every nerve a-quiver, walked deliberately in response to the request made of her. For many reasons and on numerous occasions since the mare has driven me to exasperation and she will probably do so again, but the memory of our fire-walking act makes it impossible for me to be really cross with her and I don't think I could contemplate getting rid of her.

Innate Sensitivity

If we accept the premise that horses are non-aggressive animals it is reasonable to suggest that they have a greater sensitivity to pain, and consequently a lower pain tolerance, than those of an opposite nature. This innate sensitivity plays an important part in our relationship with horses and to a degree allows us to control these large creatures.

We have seen that, despite size and strength, the horse is a timorous fellow equipped only to run away from danger. The dog on the other hand, who has far less strength, has a very different nature. If something rustles in the bushes a dog will have his hackles up in a trice and be ready for a fight. At one time, dogs were matched against bears and even bulls, both of which they would tackle with courage and ferocity. For this reason the dog has less sensitivity than the horse and a greater tolerance of pain.

Whilst stallions will fight, the average horse, even a stallion, will rarely attack a man. We talk, loosely, about horses 'fighting' the bit. They may appear to be doing so viewed from the other end of the reins, but in fact they are doing exactly the opposite. They are, as usual, running away from the discomfort imposed upon them and the more you pull at their mouths the more urgent becomes the necessity to get away from the pain. Their reaction is to pull harder and to go faster. It may sound to be a rather thick-headed proceeding when we know that if the horse would just be sensible and stop we could give up the tug-of-war. But the horse doesn't think like this, it isn't in his nature to do so. As far as he is concerned something is hurting him, and his instincts tell him to run away from it as quickly as he can. And therein lies a simple fundamental lesson which we would do well to note: pulling provokes pulling, and force exerted by the rider is always met by a stronger force on the part of the horse. Since we have not one-tenth of the horse's strength there are no prizes for guessing who will win the contest.

Recognizing the innate sensitivity of the horse we will realize that it can be used to our advantage in teaching him to obey the hands and legs. If, for instance, we stand at the horse's head and tap his flank with our long whip he will move *away* from the very slight discomfort caused by the whip. In time, he will learn to move *away* in the same manner from the action of a single leg asking for a shift of the quarters to one side or another. Similarly, he will move forward, and *away*, from the lunge whip which threatens him from behind, even though there is no intention of his being hit with the implement.

Horses will rarely resist us deliberately unless they become confused or excited, or when the fear of a greater discomfort assumes the ascendancy.

Occasionally, a horse may seem to act contrary to his nature, as when he kicks in the stable. Some horses will kick in these circumstances for the reason that being confined in a small space no other course of defence is open to them. Feeling trapped, they can kick out if they are startled by a sudden movement behind them and some will lay back their ears and kick, usually somewhat half-heartedly, when their food is brought. Too much notice should not be taken of a horse that pulls faces at feeding times, and a growl is usually sufficient to remind him of his manners. For a moment, on these occasions, the horse is suffering from what may be termed a reversion. Food is so important to him that, just as he would threaten another horse to keep away from his food bowl when being fed outside, so he acts in the same way towards the human, whom he doesn't realize has no similar interest in the contents of the bowl. In other cases the thought of food, which is always exciting to the horse, causes excitability to a quite high degree and he expresses his anxiety by nervous kicking. Fortunately, this sort of kicking is not usually directed at the food bearer but it still needs to be checked with firmness. Excitement caused by the anticipation of food is, of course, a reason why feeding should be carried out at regular and fixed times. The longer the horse has to wait for his supper the more agitated he becomes, and even if he doesn't mean to hurt you, that will be no consolation for having received the full force of a shod hoof.

Co-operation

Whilst sensitivity plays a considerable part in training, the extraordinary spirit of co-operation to be found in the horse is in reality our greatest ally. Surprisingly, this great, timorous, highly-strung animal, so dependent upon his human master, is one of the most amenable and co-operative creatures in creation. He really likes to please and will do so if given half a chance: if, that is, his owner can be bothered to understand him and win his respect and trust. He can carry the spirit of co-operation to extremes and, having learnt a movement, will accept his rider's wishes. I remember one horse who had difficulty in understanding that I wanted him to cross his legs and proceed laterally in a few steps of half-pass. Eventually the penny dropped and we obtained the required movement, whereupon he was made much of and rewarded. For some three weeks thereafter I hardly dared to move a leg or shift my weight in the saddle. He was so pleased with himself that the slightest movement on my part sent him gaily into half-pass wherever we happened to be. Even today my daughter's pony, whom, very unwisely, I taught to bow, will drop to one knee if a hand (or even a toe!) should touch his elbow.

Without this endearing quality how far would we get with our horses?

Courage

Finally, we come to the last of our sub-headings, the quality of courage, the most priceless gift we can receive. It is almost unbelievable that an animal like the horse can possibly be courageous, but he is. In part the veneers of training, overlaying and subduing the inherent instincts will allow the horse to overcome his natural fears even to the point where he disregards the fundamental instinct of self-preservation. But it is only in part; without courage would he jump fences without knowing what awaited him on the landing side, would he cross boggy ground when every instinct he possesses tells him of its danger, would he, indeed, face the terror of heavy traffic or, like my mare, walk through the smoke of a lighted fire? I doubt it. Nothing is more true than that a bold rider makes a bold horse, but how often is the boot on the other foot?

The Memory

These, then, are some of the factors contributing to the nature of the horse but he has other attributes, not the least of which is his prodigous and uncannily retentive memory. We make use of it in every aspect of training but we should recognize that it is a two-edged sword, for the horse remembers both good and bad. In our dealings with him we write as on stone and what is written remains, for better or worse, forever.

As we have seen, the horse is incapable of reason, he cannot be threatened, like a child, with the withholding of a sweet unless he behaves, nor can he be bribed. Such treatment is outside his comprehension. But he does have the power to associate cause and result which are closely related in terms of time. If he does something well and is rewarded immediately he associates the particular action with the pleasurable experience of reward, he remembers when he is asked to do it again and he knows that he has earned our approval. Conversely, if he kicks and receives summary and swift retribution for his sin he associates the kick with something unpleasant and will be deterred from giving a repeat performance.

What he does not understand is delayed punishment, or reward. It is no good after a disastrous round in the show-jumping ring, replete with every form of refusal and evasion, taking him back to his box and giving him a good belting. Too great a time has elapsed between the crime and the punishment for him to associate the one with the other, even if such punishment could be justified, which it can't, and he will become confused and resentful at the injustice perpetrated upon him. Punishment or reward must be immediate if either are to be effective. This leads us to a consideration of those two frequently misunderstood actions.

Reward and Punishment

If we are honest we must admit that horses are trained to a very large extent by the use of both reward and punishment. Centuries ago the accent was on punishment, it being considered sufficient reward when the punishment stopped. Today, we are more knowledgeable, more considerate and more humane – although whether *all* horses and ponies would agree is another matter. Punishment, indeed, is too strong a word. The basis of training, apart from our understanding of the physical and mental limitations of our pupil, rests on a system of reward and minimal, momentary discomfort, the latter, as the training develops, being made continually less apparent by a willingness on the part of the horse to respond. As an example we can think of one way in which our legs are used. They act by being closed briefly on the horse in order to produce movement (by being applied in this way they represent a minimal discomfort) and they yield when the horse obeys and moves forwards (by this yielding action the discomfort is removed and the horse is, therefore, rewarded).

We misunderstand the system when we think of rewards in terms of continual sugar lumps and discomfort in terms of the whip. This is not to say that the sugar lump should never be given nor that the whip should never be used. There is a place for the sugar, but it should be used with discretion lest it loses its appeal. Next to the return to stable, it is the greatest reward we can bestow, and should be treated as such. In other respects, the pat, the soft word, the relaxation allowed after a few minutes of hard work and, above all, the immediate yielding of hand and leg the moment obedience is obtained, in these we can be generous to a fault and no harm will be done. Likewise there will be occasions when the whip must be used to correct an unruly horse. It would not be natural if your youngster was not naughty sometimes and we must recognize that individual horses can be awkward and sometimes plain cussed.

The difficulty for the trainer is to know when a horse is being bloodyminded, which can happen, and when he is just confused and does not understand. In the latter case, which is the most frequent, it is we who are at fault and deserve the whip, not him. Just occasionally, however, we will come up against a young gentleman who has got too big for his boots and, after giving him the benefit of the doubt on one or two occasions, we may need to give him a good slap on his bottom. That should be sufficient – that and no more. More usually we will correct far less violently. A growl or a sharp word is usually sufficient to check incipient misbehaviour, and an extra squeeze with the leg, supported if necessary by a quick rat-a-tat with the heels and then, if need be, a tap with the whip, will be enough to obtain obedience to the aids given. The great thing is to ensure that you are always in a position to reward and never in one where vigorous correction is needed.

We shall aim through the training of the young horse to obtain response to aids which continually decrease in the strength and duration of their application. Ultimately we want our horse to respond to the slight shift of the leg and the gentlest squeeze of the fingers on the reins. If we keep this object in mind we shall find as we progress that the strength of our corrective actions will be reduced in like measure.

Now whilst it is obviously essential to appreciate how the mind works we should not overlook the fact that it is a small mind, incapable of concentration for any long period. Nothing is more calculated to produce a sulky, dull horse, or one that resists habitually, than working beyond his limited mental capacity. He just cannot concentrate indefinitely and work, as opposed to exercise, must be of short duration plentifully sprinkled with periods of rest. Similarly, work must be varied, otherwise the horse will soon enough become bored with it and we shall lose his attention.

The Senses

To complete the personality of the horse we are left with the five senses plus one more, the extra sixth sense of heightened perception which, in the horse, is just as apparent as the more familiar Taste, Touch, Smell, Sight and Hearing.

Taste in the horse is, one imagines, much the same as in any other animal and has little relevance to training beyond the fact that we know that the horse enjoys a sweet titbit, relishes honey or molasses in his feed and appreciates the succulence of an apple, carrot or a mangel.

Touch seems to have a little more significance, since the horse will often appear to gain assurance by touching the first pole we lay on the ground for him to walk over with his foot, and having done so will cross over it and the ones that follow without trouble. He will also touch objects with his nose, but then his sense of smell, a highly developed one, will be employed also.

Horses use their noses very considerably. They are able to scent other horses quite a long way off and if there were any mountain lions and the like still about they would smell them pretty quickly, too. One horse of mine would get very upset, even to breaking out in a sweat, at the smell of blood from a nearby food factory fitted with its own abattoir. I rarely rode him within two miles of the place but if the wind was towards us he would pick up the scent and become very frightened. Occasionally when hunting we would have to pass closer and although he would go on with the other horses he would never settle on those days. I think all horses have an aversion to the smell of blood, although I know many in hunt kennels, where slaughtering is commonplace, who seem to have become accustomed to it. What is, I am sure, certain is that horses smell human fear, as well as sensing its presence in other ways, and that it produces a corresponding emotion in themselves. Human fear, resulting in a body moisture, has a distinct smell. My own olefactory organ is not sufficiently sensitive to have experienced it but I have it on very good authority, from a Dyak tracker who would run nose-down on a trail through thick jungle, that humans do exude a particular and recognizable odour when frightened. The old horse-tamers certainly believed it and put an aromatic fluid on their hands that was supposed to bring quiet to the most savage breast, and I see that even today a similar fluid is advertised for dealing with unruly horses. My own horses seem to appreciate my after-shave lotion first thing in the morning, particularly if it is one of the very expensive ones I sometimes get for Christmas.

That the horse has remarkable eyesight is undeniable but we should remember that it is very different to our own. His eyes do not, generally speaking, focus together on objects directly in front of him, but he has the ability to see to each side and, if he raises his head, even behind him. But he can't see in his manger and it is unlikely that he ever sees his own feet, a deficiency he shares with certain humans if not for the same reason. This all-round vision is part of his protective equipment but it can make things difficult for him when jumping if his rider does not recognize his mount's limitations. By moving his head and neck the horse adjusts his vision. When jumping, he places his head so that his eyes can both see the fence at about a 15-yard distance. Four feet from the fence the lower part of his head makes the use of two eyes simultaneously impossible, so he tilts the whole head to one side and uses just one eye. He can only do this if his rider allows him sufficient freedom of head and neck. Horses strapped down with martingales, or forced by ignorant hands to move with their head hauled up in the sky, just can't see what they are expected to jump let alone make any judgement of distance. They are forced to jump blind, and that is neither a safe proceeding nor one likely to ensure a clear round.

Hearing is similarly highly developed, indeed there is a theory that a horse, whose head is rather like a sound-box, 'hears' through his feet, by vibrations, as well as through his ears. Because his hearing is so acute and because, too, he can recognize the tone of our voice, he is particularly responsive to it. It is the first of our 'aids' and a very valuable one, through which we can soothe the flighty, command the attention of the inattentive, liven the sluggard and rebuke the wrong-doer.

Incidentally, the ears tell us a great deal. Laid back they are a warning of temper, pricked forward they reveal an interest in something in front of them and sometimes, in consequence, a lack of attention to our commands. Ideally, we want the ear nearest to us, if we are schooling from the ground, to be constantly flicking back and forth to assure us of the horse's attention. When riding, the ears should act in like manner, always listening for our voice.

Lastly, there is that strange sixth sense that allows the horse to assess the mood of his rider and by which he becomes the mirror of the man who sits on him. The horse is acutely sensitive to atmosphere and responds accordingly. Whether he sees those things outside human ken I do not know but that he perceives instantly timidity, hesitation, irritability and anger as well as confidence and courage in the human is certain beyond doubt.

I have sketched, admittedly in some detail, an outline of the horse's personality – it is, even so, not necessarily complete and we shall find that it varies in one aspect or another from horse to horse. If by understanding the horse's make-up we begin to realize the handicaps with which he has to contend we shall be in a better position to cope with the problems that are bound to arise as we set out on our training programme.

Chapter 3   Choosing a Horse

If you have bred a foal of your own, and intend to start his training as a three-year-old, the problem of choice does not arise, and the animal will, presumably, have been well-fed and handled from the beginning of his life.

If we are not in this position and are in the market for a suitable young horse to bring on, we should consider carefully the type of horse we want to acquire, paying particular attention to his conformation, temperament and the way in which he has been reared.

Training a young horse is an expensive business in terms of both cash and time; also a considerable risk is involved. We can be put to no little loss, for instance, if our young horse should develop some unsoundness which makes the continuation of his training impossible. To be entirely realistic, it is just not worth expending effort, time and money on an animal whose deficiencies in conformation will make it impossible to reach our objectives in the training progression. Intelligent schooling will improve the horse, certainly, but unless his physical proportions are good he will never become anything more than a mediocre performer and he may be more disposed towards unsoundness. There will be exceptions to this rule, of course, but there is no way of knowing at the outset whether the oddly-shaped youngster will turn out to be a top-class show-jumper. He may, but it is safer to assume that he won't. The ideal subject should also be blessed with an equable temperament. It is possible to make a superficial assessment in this regard but otherwise, alas, we must take a gamble in this department and hope that our original impression was the right one.

A horse that is unsound before he has started to work is only likely to get worse as time goes on and he should be avoided at all costs.

Apart from the horse's mental outlook, about which we shall be little the wiser after the brief acquaintance that is available to us, it is conformation that sets the limits on performance and, when buying, it is to this that we should pay the greatest attention.

It is not nearly so easy to judge the make and shape of a

young horse as it is to appreciate that of the one who has reached maturity. What we have to do is to imagine what the horse is going to look like two years hence, mentally super-imposing the muscular development of the mature horse on the young frame before us. Essentially, at this stage we are looking for good proportions and a natural balance in a horse displaying no obvious deficiencies in the former respect. A horse with a heavy forehand and possibly a big, coarse head will never, whatever we do, become a balanced ride; he will always carry too much weight on the front end. On the other hand, an inclination to poor, mean quarters with the tail held low and probably a pair of weak-looking hindlegs into the bargain is just as bad and should be discarded accordingly. We shall improve his quarters by gymnastic exercises but it will be impossible to transform them into a highly efficient propulsive unit. Similarly, ewe-necks and those of the very short, thick variety are best avoided. Pay, also, particular attention to feet and limbs; armies may march on their stomachs but horses walk, trot and gallop on legs and feet. Uneven feet, contracted heels, dropped soles and very thin ones, predispose their owner to unsoundness, and any animal whose feet offend in any of these respects should be rejected.

As a very rough guide, disregarding the fact that a young horse will naturally be lower at the wither than at the croup, check that the withers are well defined then make a rough estimate of the length of the back from the rear of the withers to the croup, and of the distance between the point of the shoulder and the last of the false ribs (there are eight true ribs beginning at the front of the structure followed by ten false ones). The former measurement should be short and the last one long. The greater the difference between the two, the better is the overall proportion of the horse.

Now look at the way the horse carries his head and tail at a free trot. His head carriage at this pace will approximate pretty closely, allowing for further development, to that which will be obtained under saddle when he is trained. A tail carried normally indicates that there is nothing which will prevent the development of a good, round top line. One that is carried very high (except in the case of the Arab) or clamped firmly between the buttocks reveals that somewhere along the back there is a particular stiffness. Any damage or congenital mal-formation in this area at this age is a bad omen for future development. We shall have problems enough with our young horse without buying them ready-made.

Even a short examination of our intended purchase should reveal to us how well he has been reared and handled, but there is no harm in doing what we can to find out as much as possible about the horse's background before leaping into a motor-car to travel half-way across the country to see him.

The better a horse is fed between birth and the age of three the greater will be his development. Failure in this respect is never made up in later years, the child being very much the father of the man in the equine context. Obviously, it is not possible to outdo nature, but good and plentiful feeding of the youngster will ensure his reaching his full potential. If you buy a weedy, little three-year-old don't delude yourself by thinking that he will be alright when you have stuffed him full of food – you will only be disappointed when he grows into a weedy, under-sized five-year-old. The importance of young stock being given a good start cannot be emphasized too much. Up to the age of three a young horse should have the freedom of ample, good grazing and, in addition, he should be afforded the company of his own kind so that he develops naturally and fully. Also, he needs supplementary feeding to attain his full growth. As a guide a foal can be given 1 lb of concentrates for each month of his age up to a maximum of 5–6 lb, according to his size. These feeds will consist of nuts or cubes, bran, oats, linseed, apples, carrots etc., and can also include a little powdered milk (2–8 oz per day) and a ration of cod-liver oil, in one form or another, which will promote bone growth. As well as the concentrates, a young horse requires hay, at least from September to the Spring. The sort of hay to feed to young animals is the best quality meadow hay, which is softer and more easily dealt with by young mouths.

At two years the ration of concentrates will be increased by about 1 lb, or more for bigger horses, and at three the horse ought to be in receipt of a 9 lb daily ration divided into three feeds. A properly-managed three-year-old should also have been handled. His feet will have been attended to regularly and, making allowances for occasional youthful exuberances, he ought to lead well enough in hand from his headcollar.

Quite early in his life he will have been accustomed to the stable and will most probably have lived in during the Winter nights. On this assumption it can be taken that he is quite happy to be caught in his field. Such an association with the ways of man will have laid a very sound foundation for future training and will save an awful lot of time.

If the horse we are thinking of buying has been shown in-hand, this, too, will be an advantage, since it follows that he must have been introduced to a box or trailer. If this is so, we shall be saved the task of teaching him how he is expected to behave in this respect. I say that this will be an advantage but, of course, it could prove to be just the opposite. It all depends on how this early training has been carried out. All too frequently a singular lack of intelligence is displayed about loading an animal into a box – take a look at the horse lines of any show and you will see some shining examples.

Properly done from the beginning, there need be no difficulty and it need never enter the youngster's head that boxing is something to be resisted. But how often do we see people trying to load a mare and foal and endeavouring to persuade the mare to enter the box first? The idea is that where the mare goes the foal will follow, which is fine, except that the mare won't leave her foal! She then plays up, the foal follows suit, and we have encouraged in it a disobedience which need never have arisen. The sensible way to box a mare and foal is to put the foal in first; then the mare will quickly follow. If the foal is cradled between the arms of two helpers, each having one arm round the foal's back-end and one of them holding the end of the mare's lead in that hand, the foal can be bundled in with the minimum of trouble and the mare will follow on. In this way the foal is never given a bad example to copy.

A similar lack of intelligence on the part of the human is revealed by a head-shy youngster, who has probably become so by having a headcollar forced on to his head as a baby. All that was necessary was to position the foal correctly when giving him his first halter lesson. If he had been placed with an assistant cradling his quarters and then urged forward into an open foal slip held by another helper so much trouble could have been avoided. However, we will hope that the youngster we select has not been treated unintelligently.

Finally, the breeding of the horse will depend to a great extent on personal preference, but we would be well advised not to over-horse ourselves at this stage or any other.

A Thoroughbred will most probably have good conformation and balance and some of them are very quick on the uptake – an advantage to the highly-skilled trainer but sometimes the opposite for the beginner. On the other hand, one is more likely to find the scatty, out-and-out neurotics in the Thoroughbred category. They are, of course, highly couraged and possibly more temperamental than animals of less aristocratic descent. Consequently, to produce them really well calls for experience on the part of the trainer and a very calm outlook. In general, the beginner will probably be better with something less highly bred although these too present particular problems. Half-breds and less can be slow and dull and horses of this type are probably just as difficult to train, since it is so easy to fall into the trap of hurrying them.

My advice to the beginner would be to choose a horse with some proportion of pony blood. They usually inherit good sense and are yet quick on the uptake.

Pure-bred Arabs I regard as being difficult subjects, for the good reason that I don't seem to get on with them, although I very much like the Anglo-Arabs and some of the part-breds. The pure-bred Arab is certainly intelligent, as far as we can apply this word to the horse, but he often has a decided mind of his own which is not always in accordance with my ideas of what he should be doing. It may be, of course, that it is just my sense of humour that is at fault.

Does the sex of the animal make any difference? Well, the answer is that it can in certain individuals. The stallion apart, mares are usually, but not always, more temperamental than geldings and become more so when in season. The gelding, unaffected by sexual considerations, is more often the easier to train, although this will not always be the case. A young gelding always reminds me of a bumbling, gauche and over-grown schoolboy, subject to much the same high spirits on occasions as his human counterpart. He can, however, be corrected, possibly by a slap on his bottom, without becoming resentful. I think one has to be rather more careful and subtle with the mare.

Temperament, as I have said, is difficult to assess, but the extremes are always evident. On the whole the best advice that can be given is not to buy a horse whose personality doesn't appeal immediately. A professional trainer of horses must take them as they come but the amateur can afford to be more choosy. If training is going to be fun for both horse and human then it seems to me that your horse should be one that you really like. I don't think I have ever come across a horse that aroused my active dislike but I have met some whose characters just didn't appeal to me. Possibly, the feeling was mutual, but it could hardly be regarded as a promising basis for partnership. Few people would think of entering a business venture with a partner they didn't like and the same surely applies when choosing an equine partner. Horses, like people, are not all angels and it must be recognized that some of them will have temperaments which, though they may provide a challenge to the very dedicated, will be a constant exasperation to those with less experience. There are, in fact, neurotic animals, just as there are neurotic humans. There may be good reasons for their condition but these horses are not suitable subjects for beginners, and will, indeed, not be very economical ones for anyone else either. We may, unavoidably, become lumbered with the occasional human neurotic, and that is trying enough, but it is asking for trouble to enter, voluntarily, into partnership with one, whether human or equine.

Having taken a look at the qualities we hope to find in our ideal young horse, in the following chapter we will look at the other side of the coin and examine the qualities and skills necessary for the human end of the partnership.

Chapter 4　The Ideal Trainer

Right at the beginning of this short but important chapter let me say that the trainer I am going to describe will not be found on this earth. He is a cross between a saint and a genius and you are unlikely to meet one of this breeding. (On reflection, I doubt if we have missed much; can you not imagine how insufferable such a paragon would be?) Nevertheless, it is worth examining the attributes of the perfect trainer if only to recognize our own shortcomings.

1　The purely physical requirements of a trainer are that he should be a capable, effective rider, not necessarily a lightweight, and that he should be reasonably fit. Even more important is that he should be an 'educated' horseman, which is not quite the same thing as being capable and effective. To be an educated horseman carries the implication that the rider has taken the trouble to learn and has acquired a sound knowledge of both the theory and practice of equitation. Once more, it is impossible to teach what you don't know. If you don't know clearly what it is you are aiming at, you cannot hope to produce it. The language of communication between horse and man has to be learnt by the human, first, before he, in turn, can teach it to the horse.

As a rider, the trainer should have reached the stage where the security of his seat is taken for granted and where his aids, and the application of them, have become a matter of second nature. To have reached this point is not just a matter of experience. There are many people who have ridden for years and yet are quite incapable of positioning their horses. This may work perfectly well on a made hunter in the hunting field but it's no good if you want to train a young horse. In a nutshell, the trainer must not only have experience but must, also, have learnt to ride until his aids are applied as automatically as most of us change gear in our motor-cars. The great advantage of the educated horseman is that he will have at his disposal not just one, but many methods which will be applicable in certain circumstances. Thus equipped, he can select the one he thinks most suitable to overcome a difficulty and if that doesn't work he still has one or two more up his sleeve. The trainer who knows only one way to achieve an objective will soon find his meagre resources exhausted and then he is in a position of stalemate.

2   The remaining qualities of the trainer are entirely mental ones. He must, for instance, be **Intelligent**. It may sound to be a very obvious requirement, but it is a fact that for too long horses have been regarded as the province of those whose brain power is not exactly of the first order. It has to be admitted that in many cases horses are treated unintelligently, and that even normally intelligent people can be excessively stupid when dealing with equines.

3   A trainer needs to be a **Sensitive** person, not in the sense of being a delicate, hot-house plant, but having, if the description is not too pie-in-the-sky, the ability to respond to the sensitivity of the horse and to be able, almost, to *feel* the horse's mind. This influence of the mind plays a large part in the training since the horse is able to respond to the atmosphere created by his trainer. Through our minds we are able to relax the horse, enthuse him and to exert control over him. To do so, however, we must have acquired:

4   **Self-Discipline.** Until we are in command of ourselves we cannot hope to command others, be they human or equine. The person unable to control his temper or subject to black depressions has no place with horses. He will merely produce in them a reflection of his own unbalanced personality.

5   Then our perfect trainer will need **Patience** in full measure, which will be acquired with self-discipline, even if on occasions its preservation will require a considerable effort.

6   Finally, there must be present within the trainer of horses a **Positive** attitude towards his work. It is the core of steel at the centre of his being which makes his actions always decisive. A negative approach to the horse and to his training is no good at all and is entirely unproductive of results. We must, however, be positive only in the correct measure and beware that, in our efforts to be a dynamic personality, we do not take the horse along too fast. In practice such is the stress that has rightly been laid on not hurrying the horse and on the admirable paradox that you cannot hurry too slowly, that the majority of people, particularly the more gentle females, fall into the opposite error. It is possible to be too slow and over-careful. Quite a number of beginners, terrified lest they should ask too much, will spend weeks and months, and sometimes years, teaching a horse to jump a 12-inch pole in perfect style.

It is all very well, but not exactly of much use if the horse never gets beyond this stage.

Because none of us is perfect we shall make mistakes but if we start on our training with a knowledge of both our own and our horse's limitations we shall avoid making irreparable ones. If, on reaching this point, you feel utterly unable to measure up to these requirements then it is better to give up the idea of making a young horse for the time being and spend a little longer equipping yourself for the job.

For the benefit of unhorsey parents possessed of horse-mad fourteen- and fifteen-year-old females let me tell them unequivocally that, even if the little dear has been riding since she was a toddler, she is not yet fitted to be given a young horse to make for herself.

Chapter 5

Equipment and Facilities for Phase 1 (Three-Year-Old)

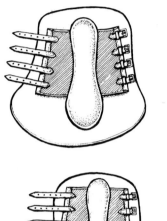

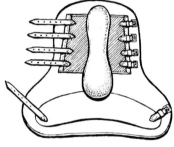

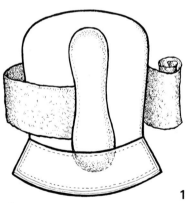

Figure 4
Types of boots suitable for use when training a young horse. The first two (fore and hind) are polo boots and the last a felt boot fastened with a bandage.

A workman is only as good as his tools. It might be reasonable to turn this saying back to front to read, with equal truth, the tools are only as good as the workman, but equipment is necessary and, also, suitable areas in which to put it to use.

Well before the young horse enters into the first stages of his programme the equipment required must be collected together and checked to make sure it is in good repair. Young horses can be very violent and we do not wish to court disaster for the sake of a few stitches or a new buckle.

Whether the first item on my equipment list can really be classified under that title is problematical, but, as this is as good a place as any, this is where it goes.

It is **an Assistant**. You can carry out the schooling on your own but it is far more satisfactory to have a helper, particularly in the early sections. This assistant must be a reliable one; the sort of person who, like a good whipper-in, is always at the right place at the right time and capable of anticipating the needs of the moment without having to be told. One that lacks horse-sense and is always getting in your way is worse than useless and you are better off without her. Above all, the greatest virtue in an assistant is the ability to keep her mouth firmly shut. Chattering women (and I am presuming our assistant will be a girl) are a trial at any time, but when dealing with young horses, that demand the trainer's whole concentration, they are an abomination!

Given that your chosen assistant has had her tongue removed, or has, at least, learnt to keep it under control, she needs to be a lightweight of the quick, wiry sort – round puddings are not best fitted to this sort of work.

Now for the inanimate equipment:

1 **A Set of Boots for the Legs.** The best type are those of the polo variety that cover the leg well down over the coronet and afford ample protection against blows. Young horses are not either sufficiently developed or co-ordinated to attempt the simplest gymnastic exercise without getting their legs into a muddle and giving one or the other of the four a good knock.

There is no point in risking blemish or injury and possible lameness on this account, and the horse should always work in protective boots during this first stage.

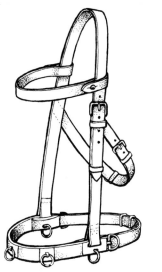

Figure 5
A useful type of lightweight lunge cavesson fitted with a stud-fastening browband and extra rings at the rear for bit- and side-reins respectively.

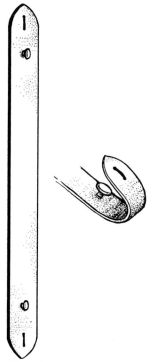

Figure 6
Detail of the stud-fastening browband recommended by the author.

2 **A Lungeing Cavesson.** Choose one of the sort illustrated with a swivelling ring on the nose, and two similar ones on either side. It is unlikely that you will need the last two but you might do and, as no saddler would consider a cavesson complete without them, you will get them, anyway. In addition have an extra pair of dees sewn on each side of the nosepiece from which a bit can be suspended by either bit straps or metal clips designed for the same purpose. Add yet another pair of dees on to the nosepiece, just above the bit dees, to which side-reins can be attached. To complete the cavesson you will need a browband, or front, but not of the conventional pattern. You need one that, instead of having the usual loop through which the headstrap passes, is made with a stud and an end which can be passed under and round the headpiece, being secured back on to the stud. Figure 5 shows a browband of this type which is, in fact, an ex-Army item and is obtainable at many saddlers who deal in ex-government equipment.

Not all cavessons are properly designed, the usual failing being the incorrect placement of the jowl strap which prevents the cheeks sliding up into contact with the eye. Make absolutely sure that the one you purchase does not fail in this respect by trying it on a horse before you buy it. Trust nothing but the evidence of your own eyes in this matter, I can assure you that the majority of cavessons on the market are not made correctly, whatever the salesman says.

3 **A Lunge Rein.** This is a fairly common piece of equipment and varies very little in design. It should be made of tubular webbing, not too heavy (you're not dealing with an elephant), and be about 35 feet long. Personally, I prefer the fastening to be of a swivel pattern so that the rein doesn't twist on itself and I like the actual attachment to the cavesson ring to be a lightweight snap hook rather than a billet and buckle.

4 **A Pair of Gloves.** Even if your lunge rein is as soft as thistle-down you will get your hands burnt painfully if a horse takes off and pulls it violently through your fingers. A pair of light hogskin gloves will prevent this happening and keep your hands clean as well.

5 **A Lunge Whip.** No lunge whip on the market has a sufficiently long thong fitted to it, but the best by a long way are those made of fibre glass or nylon. They are very well balanced and very light, and these are important considerations if a lunge whip is to be used effectively and without undue physical effort.

6 A Pair of Side-Reins. Years ago (during my 'elastic' stage) I was guilty of popularizing side reins inset with elastic or rubber inserts. I have regretted it ever since it dawned upon me that I was contributing to the great legion of horses who are perpetually behind the bit. The so-called 'give and take' action of the elastic side-rein, particularly the 'take' part, encourages the horse to evade the tension by tucking in his nose and coming out of contact with his bit. When I discovered my error I went off to find out just how side-reins should be used and was surprised to find that neither I, nor many thousands of others, have ever really understood their purpose. We shall discuss their correct use at the appropriate place, but meanwhile buy a pair of absolutely plain, very light, side-reins, with ample adjustment, and fastening to the bit and the rings of the roller with neat clip hooks.

7 A Body Roller. A good stout one is needed with well-fitted pads and adjustment at both sides for convenience and correctness of fit. It should be equipped with three large rings on each side, the lowest being about half-way down the horse's body. In addition, and for a particular purpose, I like to have a ring fitted centrally on the front of the roller and attached to it by a piece of leather about 5 inches long which can be shortened by means of a simple buckle. Some people

Figure 7
A complete breaking roller. The cut-away portion in the bellyband is to prevent galling at the elbows.

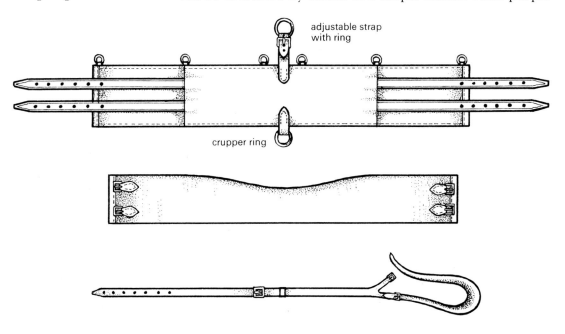

adjustable strap with ring

crupper ring

like to use a crupper to keep the roller in place but I am not really in favour of one. Properly fitted it should not cause soreness to the dock but when used with side-reins (the only valid reason for its presence) the two can induce a sort of both-ends-against-the-middle effect, resulting in a hollowing of the back – something which is the very antithesis of our ideal of the rounded top line.

You will also need a nice, soft, and fairly large pad to place under the roller pads to prevent any possibility of chafing and to give greater comfort to the horse.

Incidentally, if you have the front edge of your roller belly-band shaped to the rear so that it lies well behind the elbows you will avoid the danger of the horse being rubbed in that area should the roller slip forward.

8 A Lead Rein. A simple lead with a snap hook fastening, the whole about 8 feet long, is all that is required.

9 A Bit. The type of first bit to be used is optional. Many very experienced trainers cling to the old type of mouthing bit with keys, in either the straight bar or jointed form. The idea of the keys is that the horse plays with them, makes saliva in his mouth and is encouraged to relax his lower jaw. This is quite a viable theory but it has to be recognized that the mouthing action can also cause the horse to retract his head and get into the habit of becoming behind his bit, whereas we want him always to seek out its contact and accept it. For this reason I prefer to use a plain half-moon snaffle of either rubber or vulcanite in the first stages. I obtain a better result with this bit and this is a good reason for my using it. I do not condemn the use of the key bit but I recognize its possible disadvantages. It is absolutely essential that the bit, as well as all other equip-meny, fits perfectly. Too narrow a bit will cause discomfort and evasion, too large a one will have similar results. In the case of jointed key snaffles, most of the ones used are too large, and because of this the horse is encouraged to place his tongue over the centre joint. Once this habit becomes confirmed it is difficult to break. It is, of course, quite impossible to get a horse to respond to the bit whilst his tongue is over it. In fact, should a horse become confirmed in this habit further progressive training is out of the question.

10 A Plain Snaffle Bridle fitted with reins and a fat jointed snaffle of the German type, or with a Fulmer-type snaffle, which has cheeks and a pair of small retainers to fasten the latter to the cheeks of the bridle. At this stage a drop-noseband is not required and there is, in any case, no need to regard it as an essential part of the horse's equipment at this or any other

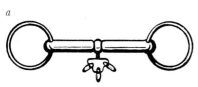
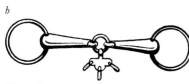

Figure 8
(*a*) Straight bar mouthing bit with keys.
(*b*) Jointed mouthing bit with keys.

Figure 9
Half-moon or mullen mouth snaffle, frequently made of rubber or vulcanite.

Figure 10
The broad-mouthed German snaffle.

Figure 11
The Fulmer cheek snaffle.

time. If we find we have need of one it will be easily obtained, but until then there is no point in buying a corrective device for a fault that hasn't arisen.

11   A Saddle. For some reason that is never clear to me people seem to think that any old saddle will do for backing. Well, it won't, so let's make sure we have the right one from the very beginning. We have already discussed the balance of the horse and the necessity for the rider to position himself correspondingly. It seems obvious, therefore, that we should use a saddle designed to put the rider's weight in line with the horse's centre of gravity and to assist the rider in maintaining that position.

Since it is very difficult for the young horse to carry weight initially, why make it more so by using a saddle which places the rider out of balance and imposes unnecessary strain on the horse?

Throw away the ancient board-like monstrosity which 'Old Charlie' always used for backing and get a good deep-seated modern saddle, possibly of the spring-tree type. It will need a pair of leathers and irons, as usual, and a girth. It is better on soft youngsters to use either a nylon girth or one made of lampwick rather than one of the leather types, which might chafe. Normally, I regard numnahs as inessentials, but in this case we can use one to ensure maximum comfort for our pupil. If he is uncomfortable in any way he will object and we shall lose his concentration – nothing must be allowed to distract him from the job in hand.

12   A Long Whip, sometimes called a dressage whip, is one of the most essential tools and no trainer should be without one.

One could include a neckstrap, for seizing in emergencies, in this list but, as the wretched things are never in the right place when wanted, it can hardly be considered essential. A piece of mane, which has the advantage of being a permanent fixture, is just as satisfactory.

All equipment must, for the reasons mentioned, fit well, be in good order and be made soft and supple before it is used.

It is quite amazing how many people, and quite experienced ones at that, neglect these elementary precautions, using old, dirty and neglected tack, and as a result create problems for themselves. Too much attention cannot be paid to the suitability of the schooling tackle, and those who ignore this basic factor are the ones who are going to be equally lax in the training that follows.

Facilities

Ideally, training facilities should include an indoor school, outdoor arenas, miles of green lanes and tracks, jumping equipment, etc. Essentially, we need an enclosed area of a reasonable size, 120 feet × 60 feet would do very well but you can manage with a smaller one, situated far enough away from the horse's box and customary field so that the latter cannot act as a distraction. If the area can be fenced round with hurdles, so that the horse cannot see through the walling, so much the better. The surface needs to be level and sufficiently well drained to be rideable in most weathers. One of rough sand, mixed with ash or peat, is usually acceptable and will provide good going.

For this stage you will not need much jumping equipment beyond half-a-dozen good stout poles, 8–10 feet long, which can either be left rough or painted in colours so that the horse gets used to the look of coloured poles early on, and a set of cavalletti (five if possible). These can be made to the dimensions in Figure 12 to give heights of 10, 15 and 19 inches.

Figure 12
Diagram showing the construction of a cavalletto and the three positions in which it may be used.

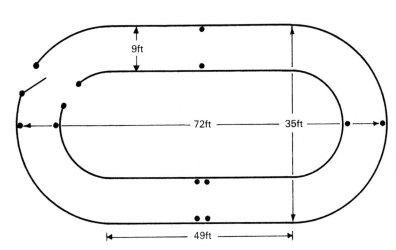

Figure 13
The ideal jumping lane.

If between the three- and four-year-old stages you win a football pool or a rich aunt dies you might like to consider the construction of a jumping lane of the type illustrated in Figure 13. This is admittedly a bit of a luxury, although a very useful piece of equipment.

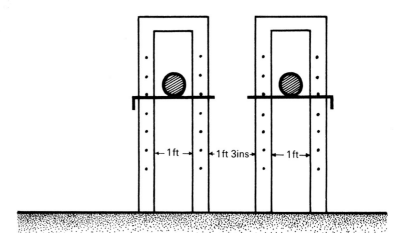

Figure 14
Method of constructing a 'fixed' spread fence for use in a jumping lane.

In the later stages of the progression some simple fences, both plain and coloured, will be necessary, but for the moment the poles and cavalletti will be adequate.

The more facilities that are available the easier is the trainer's job, but it is quite astonishing how well one can manage with quite simple arrangements and the use of imagination and ingenuity. What you cannot expect is to be able to train a horse if your only facility is an open field. An enclosure, of some kind, even if it is only a small one, is absolutely essential if the horse is to be worked without annoying distractions.

Finally, other horses must be included as a facility. Young horses learn by example and an older, steady animal can be invaluable, particularly when we reach the point of taking our pupil out hacking and in traffic.

Chapter 6

Phase 1 : Primary Stages in the Training of the Three-Year-Old

The training progression of the young horse falls into two distinct phases. The first, which we shall refer to as Phase 1, is concerned with the raw three-year-old taken up from the pasture in April and worked very lightly up to the following August. The horse is then rested until April of the following year when, in his fourth year, his secondary education, Phase 2, is commenced. No specific time can be put on this second phase but one would aim to keep the horse in work so that he could do a few half days in the hunting field throughout the season. At the end of hunting the horse will need to be given a short break at grass and thereafter such specialist education as his owner may think within the horse's capability can be undertaken. We, however, are only concerned with the periods of primary and secondary schooling.

For the sake of clarity each Phase is divided into a number of stages, but it should be remembered that there can be no strict lines of demarcation; they are part of a logical progression in which every action within the stages is a preparation for what is to follow. Everything we do and every stage is related within the progression, and whilst suggested periods of time are made, they are only suggestions. Depending upon the individual, they may quite easily take much longer, or conversely, they may be accomplished in a shorter time.

In very general terms we can liken each Phase to a kind of military exercise. The ultimate objective is defined and then the approach to that end is divided into a number of secondary objectives. Each of these, in order, must be reached and consolidated before it can be used as a base for the next leg of the operation, and so the progression continues until the final target is reached.

We shall regard our progression in the same light.

Phase 1   Stage 1

Recognizing that our three-year-old is undeveloped in mind and body the objectives we hope to achieve in Phase 1 will be directly related to these conditions. In the months of training between April and August we must aim to:

1 Accustom the horse to the acceptance of discipline and to being handled.
2 Prepare the horse physically to carry weight.
3 Teach him to *accept* weight on his back.
4 Teach him to *carry* weight, which will involve his making adjustments in his balance.
5 Teach the rudiments of control by the rider.

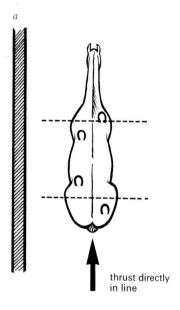

thrust directly in line

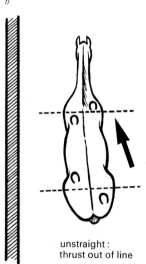

unstraight:
thrust out of line

Figure 15
The 'straight' horse (*a*) delivers the thrust of his quarters directly in line with the fall of the forefeet. The hindfeet therefore follow the track made by the forefeet. The unstraight (unschooled) horse delivers the thrust of the quarters out of line, thereby detracting from the propulsive efficiency.

The first of these are concerned with the development of the mind; the remainder are almost purely concerned with physical aspects, although the acceptance of weight combines a little of both.

Throughout Phase 1 and, indeed, during the whole training period, all our work and the methods we employ will be directed towards producing a state of **Calm** in our pupil. **Calm** is one of the three commandments at the root of all equestrian endeavour. It was General L'Hotte, one of France's greatest masters, who gave us the dictum, **Calm**, **Forward**, **Straight**, and in these three words are contained all the principles of schooling.

The state of **Calm** is clearly of vital importance since without it the horse is inattentive, unresponsive and disobedient – we can make no progress until it is achieved. When the horse is calm he can be taught to go **Forward**, a quality we shall also be looking for in Phase 1 and which implies not only instant and willing obedience to the legs but also a mental attitude. Going forward does not mean moving to the front in any old fashion. It is a definite urge displayed by the horse and is just as much a mental quality as a physical manifestation.

For a horse to be **Straight** means that because of the equal development of muscle and the flexion induced in the lumbar vertebrae of the spine by correct preparation and schooling, the congenital curve is corrected. In this state the horse's hindfeet are able to follow exactly the track made by the forefeet. He is then said to move straight. By making the horse straight we improve the mechanical efficiency of the structure, since the propulsion of the hindlegs is then delivered directly to its front and the thrust is not partially expended by being directed to one side or the other, and away from the direction of the movement (see Figure 15).

If you think that this is just unnecessary theorizing, think again, and consider why a horse is able to disobey his rider in a variety of circumstances, particularly, perhaps, when he refuses or runs out at a fence. In every case the reasons for his disobedience, apart from the considerations of unsoundness, over-facing, etc., are because (a) he ceases to go forward in response to his rider's legs, or (b) he uses his quarters, the origin of the directional movement, to frustrate his rider's intentions.

If the horse has learnt to go forward, and obeys the legs instinctively, most of our problems are removed; he cannot, for instance, stop at a fence. Secondly, if the horse is straight it must mean, inevitably, that the rider can control the position of the quarters, since we teach straightness, or at least in part, by inducing mobility in the haunches so that they can be moved at will by the action of a single leg. It follows, therefore, that the straight horse can be prevented from changing direction, through shifting his quarters, by his rider's ability to keep the latter in place and to correct any unwanted shift to either side by means of his leg. An ability to control the quarters by the legs – in combination, it must be admitted, with the aids of the hand – makes a refusal by running out a virtual impossibility.

In essence, the horse who complies with our three commandments can be positioned at will according to whatever circumstances arise. Think of the advantages of owning and riding a horse like this. Jumping – within the horse's capacity and state of training – becomes an exercise devoid of anxiety: we know that our horse will not refuse; we need have no fears about getting into trouble in a crowded lane out hunting, or in other confined spaces; and how much easier it will be to ride in traffic, secure in the knowledge that we are able to position our horse to the best advantage whatever the situation. **Calm**, **Forward**, **Straight** is not just a pleasant theory, it is a practical necessity for the all-round riding horse.

Having defined the objectives of **Phase 1** now let us consider the actual work involved in the various stages.

Stage 1 is, in fact, little more than an extension of the life the horse has so far enjoyed and will probably take up between three and four weeks. As this phase is the horse's primary school the introduction to work must be made by gradual, easy progressions which are pleasant and enjoyable.

Starting in April, when the weather should begin to be on our side and the days will be longer, the young horse can be brought into the stable to become familiar with the routine of the yard.

His food ration at this time will amount to about 9 lb of concentrates (if he has not been in receipt of so much we shall, of course, have to build up to this amount gradually) and probably 14 lb of soft meadow hay. The concentrate ration will consist, basically, of 3 lb crushed oats, 4 lb standard cubes plus 2 lb bran, which will be varied by the addition of carrots, apples, etc., and made more palatable by a sprinkling of molassine meal or a few spoonfuls of honey. The food ration should be divided into three feeds and fed slightly damp.

Linseed can be given once a week and at the weekend a good bran mash to keep his bowels in order.

It is a good idea, if it can be arranged, to put the horse out in his paddock for an hour or so during the day when the weather is anything but impossible. Not only does this practice allow the horse to stretch his legs and get rid of his high spirits but it also encourages him to relax and prevents him from becoming bored. Young horses, like young children, are quickly bored and both in this state quickly get into mischief.

My own routine during this period would be as follows, but obviously it will depend very much on the circumstances of the individual as to how the day is arranged.

7 a.m.	Quartering (i.e. a rough brush over plus cleaning of the feet); pick up droppings, etc.; first feed
8 a.m.	Mucking out, followed by grooming
9.30 a.m.	Exercise period
11 a.m.	Return to stables
1 p.m.	Second feed
2 p.m.	Horse is put out in paddock for free recreation period
4 p.m.	Horse returns to stable – 4-lb haynet
6 p.m.	Grooming and stable training
7 p.m.	Third feed
9 p.m.	Last haynet (10 lb)

The planning of a routine, however, represents nothing more than the bare bones of the exercise. The flesh which we put on the skeleton is contained in what takes place during the periods of grooming, exercise and stable training.

Grooming, apart from contributing to the health of the animal, has other benefits, not the least of which is the opportunity it affords us to develop a relationship with our pupil. In addition, if it is properly carried out, we can use it to help in the formation and build-up of muscle and, also, as a preparation for other aspects of the training with which we shall be concerned later. Bearing this in mind we should work up to grooming the horse thoroughly. I say 'work up' because it will be a gradual process. We cannot attack the young horse in his box with brush and comb and stable rubber until he has had time to adjust to his new life. If we do he will soon become nervous and irritable at our approach and we shall have lost, right at the beginning, the calm mind we are seeking to create. The state of calm, let us never forget, starts here in the horse's home and if it is not present it certainly will not come about elsewhere. So we start our grooming very gently. Even though the average youngster will have some acquaintance with the process we must not presume upon it; it will be wiser if we consider the horse as having been untouched by human hand and treat him accordingly.

Select, then, a soft brush and if he seems ticklish under his tummy or seems to resent the brush being used on his head, make use of your hand in its place. But do make sure that you groom him equally well on both sides. Most of us start grooming on the near-side and we tend in any case to continually approach the horse, even much later on in the training, from this side. *We* are then in danger of becoming *one-sided* and so, in consequence, are our horses. As often as not, therefore, start to groom on the off-side and from the start begin to rest your arm over the youngster's back to brush the opposite side. This is the first preparation for the saddle which will one day in the future be put on his back. The youngster, after a few days, should allow you to brush out his mane and tail without trouble, but do not take chances and do not brush roughly so that the hair is pulled. When brushing the tail, stand to the side; not, at first, directly behind him. The three parts to concentrate upon in these first weeks are the **Feet**, the **Head** and the **Mouth**, all of which we want to be able to handle easily.

A properly brought-up young horse should have already been made accustomed to having his feet handled and should have experienced the blacksmith attending to them. Again, however, don't take this for granted. Get into the habit of picking up the feet and cleaning them out every time you enter the box. Have the blacksmith call as soon as you can in the early days of this opening stage. But make sure your horse is prepared for his visit and will allow all his feet to be handled without his becoming silly about it. It is not a bad plan to let the young horse watch whilst an older one is being shod by the blacksmith. He will gain confidence, as is so often the case, from the good example set by his more mature companion.

Do not be afraid to spend time talking to the young horse whilst you stroke his **Head**, until after a few days he will allow you to rub his ears. Very few things can cause so much trouble as a horse that has become head-shy. By getting him used to being handled in this area we are reducing the risk of experiencing difficulty when we come to put a bridle on him.

In this respect we must also handle his **Mouth**, something which few owners think about. If we are gentle and reward the horse for his co-operation he will quickly come to accept our opening his mouth as easily as he allows us to brush his body. What is more, if we get into the habit of looking at his mouth as frequently as we pick up his feet we will be in a position to make a comparison of its condition from day to day. This is particularly important at this stage, as the horse goes through a continual process of shedding milk teeth and replacing them with permanent ones up to the age of six. Frequently during this process the gums will become inflamed and the horse, like a young child in the same circumstances, becomes fractious and irritable. Beyond rubbing the gums with tincture of myrrh or a little whisky when the inflammation is very pronounced, there is nothing much we can do for our youngster, but at least we will know why he is being irritable and will be able to make allowance for his behaviour.

If we have practised this routine of regular mouth inspection it is unlikely that we will have any trouble when we come to putting a bit in the mouth.

Before too long we shall want to be able to groom the horse without tying him up. But in the early stages it is probably easier to groom with the horse tied to a ring in the wall by a rope from his headcollar. Certainly, we shall find mucking out more easily accomplished if the horse's position is a relatively fixed one. This, however, means that we must teach the horse to stand when tied without attempting to run back. Running back on to the headcollar is something to be avoided – it quickly becomes a habit and it can result in unpleasant accidents.

There are a number of ways in which the horse can be taught to tie-up. One which is frequently used, and which probably causes more head-shy horses than any other, is to put on a really stout headcollar (it has to be very strong to withstand the weight of nearly half-a-ton of horse thrown violently against it), and to secure the horse with a virtually unbreakable rope to something like a telegraph pole. The idea is that when the horse seeks to release himself he will find himself unable to do so, however hard he fights. In the end, exhausted by his struggles, he will give in and accept defeat. It does of course work, sometimes, as do many of these strong-arm methods. At least that is, they achieve a result, but with what result and at what cost? What sort of impression do the advocates of this sort of handling think is created in the horse's mind, and is he not likely to become increasingly nervous and head-shy? This is nothing whatever to do with 'making' horses, it is purely concerned with the 'breaking' of them, and it is so unnecessary. The panic sets in when the horse feels the pressure on his head and it is then that he reverts to his wild state and fights. Calm horses do not fight, and intelligent trainers never let the horse realize how great is his own strength and how puny, in comparison, are the restraints by which the human seeks to bind him.

We can teach the horse to tie-up without frightening him and without violence. All we need to do is to take an extra long lead rope passing from his headcollar through the wall ring and back into our hand. Still holding the rope we can groom the horse and handle him. If he moves back we allow the rope to slip through the ring, then we can urge him to go forward again, perhaps with a titbit, and once more take up a light tension on the rope. Repeat this on a dozen occasions and your horse will have learnt to stand still. I have frequently spent as long as an hour sitting on a manger holding a rope in the manner prescribed and feeding the horse from my hand, encouraging him to come to me every time he took a step backwards. By the end of that time I can tie him up in the sure knowledge that he will not run back and I will guarantee that in a few days I would cure even the most confirmed breaker of headcollars by using this method. I am not trying to impress you as an omniscient trainer of horses possessed of some especial gift. I am, in fact, not particularly talented or gifted, I just use the commonsense with which I am no more plentifully endowed than anyone else.

When we have taught the horse to tie we can concentrate on teaching him how he should behave in his box, which, amongst other things, entails his beginning to learn how to move-over in response to a request from his attendant.

Initially, this can be taught by holding the horse's head inclined towards your own body and tapping his flank with a short stick or even your hand, whilst giving the command 'move-over'. The tap on the flank and the fact that his head is bent towards you ensures that he will move his quarters away. Follow this movement by having an assistant hold the head, inclining it as before, whilst the trainer stands a little in advance of the hip and taps and commands as before. Gradually, the trainer will be able to change his position and stand further away almost in line with the dock, dispensing with the tap on the flank. The same result can be obtained without an assistant, should one not be readily available, by the trainer using in the first stages the lead rope from the headcollar. In a very short time the rope will not be needed. The secret lies in positioning yourself correctly.

The horse must know to which side you want him to move and it is only indicated to him by your position. It is no good at all standing directly behind the horse and saying 'move-over'. He doesn't understand you in the first place and if he did you have not told him which way you want him to move. Indeed, the only reaction you may get from him is a kick and quite honestly you will deserve it. Much, much later, you will be able to pass safely round the back of your horse and get him to move by a click of the tongue and a pat from the appropriate hand. But at this stage don't risk it. Your young horse is not yet experienced enough for such liberties and to make him understand you must be very definite and deliberate in your movements.

An annoying little habit which can be nipped in the bud at this stage is that of moving towards the door when brought in after exercise just when you want to remove a headcollar, or just after you have taken it off. One then has to push the horse out of the way in order to leave the box. Always position the horse in the same spot, away from the door, when you bring him in, and insist upon his staying there, putting him back into position if he moves, until you are ready to leave. This is just teaching respect and good manners. For myself I do not tolerate a horse bumbling round the box whilst I am attending to him. When he is the sole occupant of his stable he may move where he will; when he shares it with me I want him to understand that it is I who dictate his movements – a little thing, but one of the first lessons in respect and discipline. Do not neglect these small things: if our horse is obedient to us in these he will be obedient when we ask more of him.

In Stage 1 we shall not require to go much further than this as far as grooming and stable training goes. It is really a period for making friends with our horse and once more you will not be wasting time if you spend half-an-hour a day doing nothing more than having a chat with him. In fact, with a nervous subject we may have to spend much longer getting him to accept our presence in the box and winning his confidence.

Similarly, the exercise period will be just as undemanding. The periods will, in fact, involve nothing much more than quiet walks, the horse being led about the place, seeing what goes on, watching other horses at work and observing the general life that goes on around him. For these walks the horse can wear his lunge cavesson fitted with the browband. As he is accustomed to a headcollar the fitting of the cavesson should present no difficulty, and since the browband can be put in place without the whole cavesson having to be pushed over his ears this, too, will cause no trouble.

Nonetheless, by wearing the browband the horse gets used to its presence and is prepared for the fitting of a normal bridle. In fact, in a very short space of time we will be able to undo the nose and jowl straps of the cavesson and then slip the headpiece gently over his ears. Make sure that, if anything, the browband is a little big rather than too small. A tight browband pulls the headpiece against the back of the ears causing discomfort which may get the horse into the habit of head-shaking – one that is most difficult to eradicate.

Lead the horse with a lunge rein from the centre ring on the nosepiece, holding the rein some 30 inches down its length and passing the remainder across the body where it can be held neatly looped in the outside hand. Let him walk on slightly in front of you, positioning your body at his shoulder. From the beginning always carry your long whip in your out-

6 Ready for his morning walk

side hand, and always lead equally from *both* sides, so that there is no encouragement for the horse to become confirmed in a permanent bend to one side or the other.

We shall not in this stage expect the horse to walk in-hand as perfectly as we shall require later on, but we can lay the foundations. To start with, we may need our assistant to follow the horse behind, particularly when we are leaving the stable, so that she can urge him to go forward. He can also learn about the whip, which we can use behind our back to tap him gently as we give the order to 'Walk–March'. We can also introduce him to a very important word in the training vocabulary – 'Whoa', which we will say every time we bring him to halt. If he stands still, rooted to the spot, as young horses do, we will **not** indulge in a fruitless tug-of-war which we cannot in any case win, but, instead, we will just step away a stride or two, moving ourselves in line with his hip and, by showing him the whip, make him circle round us. Once he is moving we can easily straighten him up and proceed on our way. He may try to make off, although this is unlikely to be more than a half-hearted attempt, in which case we shall be glad of the length of our lunge rein, since again we shall be able to make him circle us.

More than this we do not want in Stage 1, and we should be satisfied if, at the end of three weeks or so, the horse will walk along calmly with us and can be led from either side.

If difficulty is experienced at this stage and we find the horse has very little idea of leading, we can teach him what is wanted in the box. Place the horse against the wall with the trainer at his shoulder and the assistant lying handy to the rear but clear of his heels. On the trainer giving the command 'Walk–march', followed by a tap with the whip, the assistant can move up to urge the horse forward until he will walk round the box freely. He should have been taught this as a foal but if he doesn't walk in-hand, he probably hasn't, and we have to remedy the defect. There should be no trouble in taking the horse to his field for his recreational period but he might not be quite so keen to return to his stable. This can be overcome by getting a helper to get behind him again, or, if his companion is older and can be caught up first, leading him towards the gate when the youngster will invariably follow.

Throughout Stage 1, and indeed always, we should move quietly and deliberately about the yard and in the stable. But quietly and deliberately is not synonymous with 'pussyfooting' about the place as though in a sick-room.

Noise is a part of life and contributes to it if kept within acceptable proportions. We must get used to it and so must our horses. I know of one lady, a very great international horsewoman, who positively encourages the dropping of

7 Later in training the young
horse becomes accustomed to
wearing a roller

buckets and the clanging of barrows because, as she points
out in her forthright way, somebody at some time is going to
make sudden noises like this and she doesn't want her horses
to jump out of their skins every time they hear one. She has
a point there. Certainly, I think it is a very good idea to have
a radio going in the stable area, and even in the box. Horses
seem to like music (mine are good enough to make no objection to my singing voice, which is execrable) and without
doubt the present-day 'pop' music must be considered a very
good preparation for any noise, from a supersonic boom to
a pneumatic drill.

The second Stage in Phase 1 builds upon the progress made
in the first, continuing and blending with the initial introduction to schooling. Whatever else you do, do not make the mistake of saying, 'today I will teach A', or 'tomorrow I will teach
B'. You can't do it. It is an excellent thing to make a plan but
a foolish one to make a rigid plan. You must be flexible within
a general framework, appreciating that 'stages' are made only
for *our* convenience and are in fact part of a continual and
overlapping progression.

Having made a painless introduction to school we can now
begin to teach our pupil the three Rs which will culminate in
his being backed and ridden.

Chapter 7   Phase 1 Continues

In the weeks following Stage 1, *work* is gradually introduced into the *exercise* period and we should be clear of the difference between the two. Work takes place over short periods with frequent rests; exercise is not so strenuous and has a longer duration. Both are essential in the training of the horse, and both contribute to his education. If anything, it is more difficult to strike a balance between the two in these early stages than it is later on, when the horse is backed and school work and exercise are more easily defined.

Once the horse is in work and indeed in the first four weeks or so of the acclimatization period other factors will also arise which will demand our constant attention. Each day we must examine our horse carefully to ensure that he has sustained no injuries, that no incipient unsoundness is making itself apparent and that he is maintaining and improving his condition. Rations must be altered if it seems necessary and we should keep an ever-watchful eye on his health and outlook. Apart from the physical strains imposed on him we must recognize that the mental effort alone will be tiring. If he is physically fit but is dull and listless, or, conversely, irritable and inattentive in his work, it means that we are going too fast and overburdening him mentally. The answer is to stop there and then, and give the horse a few days' rest and an opportunity to relax.

Stages 2 and 3 continue the stable training and introduce the first real work preparatory to lungeing. Both these stages are of short duration, possibly as little as a week for each, but they are nevertheless essential to the progression.

Stage 2

In the stable we should now be in a position to groom the horse without his being tied, and we can begin to tidy him up by pulling his mane and tail. If this is done quietly, pulling out no more than a few hairs each day, the horse is unlikely to object. Unfortunately, far too many people, when confronted with a bushy tail, lose all sense of proportion and are determined to finish the job there and then. Not surprisingly the horse's dock will be made very sore and we cannot blame him if he is reluctant to submit to the experience in the future. Be content, therefore, with pulling half-a-dozen hairs at a time, then damp the tail and put on a tail bandage. This will involve your standing behind the horse, a proceeding which should not involve any danger at this point. If, however, you have doubts on this score, get a helper to pick up a foreleg, holding the toe between finger and thumb on the first two or three occasions. It is not very sensible to leave the bandage on all night nor to put it on so tightly as to cause discomfort. In the last instance the hairs will be broken to the detriment of the tail's appearance and the pressure will interfere with the circulation. Under these circumstances a horse will soon contract the habit of rubbing his tail against the door or manger in his efforts to rid himself of the annoyance. He is likely to do much the same thing if the bandage is left in place throughout the night. In fact, if the bandage is properly put on and is not too tight it will not stay in position until the morning. There is, therefore, no good reason for the practice. It is more satisfactory to put a tail bandage on for an hour or two each day.

Also it is a good idea to get the horse used to wearing his exercise boots by letting him wear them for an hour or so in his box before he is required to work outside in them. To start with the unfamiliar feel of the boots will cause him a little anxiety, and he may walk round his box with his hind-legs being lifted high in the air as though suffering from stringhalt (the nervous disease which causes the leg to be snapped up almost to the belly at each stride). He may even indulge in a kick or two to express his resentment, but after a little while he will take no notice of his new boots, and when he goes out there will be no fear of his being distracted by them.

In a fairly short time the horse will need shoeing, and during this stage we should prepare him by stepping up the attention given to his feet in the box until we can spend a few moments every day tapping each foot with a hammer. The act of being shod is a strange and even frightening experience for the young horse and there is no point in risking a battle royal – which may have disastrous after-effects over a long period – for the want of a little commonsense preparation. In this, as in every other aspect of the training, we must conform to the rule of preparing the horse for every successive action, so that everything falls into the natural and almost imperceptible progression we have planned – at all costs we must avoid abrupt transitions. They only serve to destroy the calm acceptance of new movements and experiences which we are forever seeking to instil into our pupil.

Finally, bearing in mind that we shall soon want to put a

saddle on our horse's back, we can take the first steps towards achieving this particular watershed.

Start by rolling up lengthways two good large sacks, securing the ends with binder twine and using the roll initially in the place of a stable rubber. Within a day or so it will be possible to lay the sack over the withers and then to ease it back until it occupies the place where ultimately the saddle will lie. Leave it there whilst the grooming continues, occasionally, with the help of an assistant, giving it a fairly strong downward pull on each side. In nine cases out of ten there will be no reaction on the part of the horse, and we can then carry the exercise a little further by weighting each end with a quantity of sand and leaving the roll in position during the grooming periods. The whole operation is unlikely to take more than thirty minutes, but it is valuable because we have taught the horse the first lesson in accepting weight on his back.

Exercise and Work

To date we shall have contented ourselves with walking the horse out, showing him his new world and not being too concerned providing he was prepared to walk along fairly quietly and could be led from either side. Now, he must learn to **walk in-hand**, which in its correct form bears little resemblance to the displays most of us associate with this simple exercise.

Whilst writing this book I was giving a course of talks on the training of the young horse, one of the earlier sessions being devoted to this work in-hand. On the day on which I intended to discuss this particular subject a lady telephoned me to ask what it was about. 'Is it very elementary?' she asked, 'you see we are just going to start lungeing our horse and I thought this was one talk we could miss as it hasn't very much to do with lungeing, has it?' I tried to explain that walking in-hand had everything to do not only with lungeing but with riding, too, and that it was as much a part of a training progression as anything else. 'You can't,' said I, 'isolate particular aspects, removing them from the context of the whole.' Of course, it was in vain, the lady didn't turn up that evening, but the following week she was at the hall early with numerous tales of woe. The horse just wouldn't work on the lunge, he kept turning round and as yet had not completed anything approaching even one circle. With some unholy joy I was able to say, 'Well, perhaps it is because he is insufficiently prepared, has he, for instance ever been taught to walk in-hand?

Walking in-hand teaches obedience to the word of com-

8 First lessons in teaching the horse to walk in hand

mand, respect (not fear) of the whip, and sets the foundation for forward movement, the second of General L'Hotte's commandments.

Already, our pupil should have a fair idea of what is wanted but there is no harm in recapitulating the lessons he has learnt so far. Again, therefore, we shall position him against a wall or hedge to prevent his swinging away from us, and we shall stand, as before, at his shoulder with our outside hand holding the long whip behind our back. Our assistant will stand ready behind the horse moving forward as the horse responds to our command 'Walk–March', which will be accompanied by a tap on the flank with our whip. During the walk we require

9 The horse moving forward in hand with a good active walk

the horse to move boldly and freely to his front whilst we remain at his shoulder, allowing and encouraging him to stretch his neck forward without restriction from the rein. Should he hesitate, a click of the tongue and the application of the whip combined with a diplomatic movement from our assistant will be enough to send him on. In this way we are implanting the idea of moving freely and vigorously forward, but under control, and the horse is learning the meaning of both the verbal command and that given by the tapping whip, which one day will be replaced by a leg. Even at this early stage we should not lose sight of our aim to produce a rounded top line giving tension to the back. For this reason it is absolutely essential to allow the horse sufficient freedom of head and neck, continually urging him to move forward into contact with our hand. We shall be trying to accomplish the same thing under saddle and the sooner the horse develops the urge to seek contact with our hand, whether wearing a cavesson or a bridle, the quicker will his progress be. The horse is not going forward, or not correctly, if the restraint imposed by the hand is too great and he carries his head twisted inwards with his nose in the air. Such a position leads inevitably to similar resistances being made under saddle. It is necessary to recognize that the influence of the hand is just as important whether it holds a rein attached to a bit, or a lunge line attached to a cavesson and it must act in the same manner, following always the movement of head and restraining by intermittent tensions applied by the fingers.

To halt the horse at walk involves the use of the body, hand, whip and voice. The trainer lengthens his stride to bring his

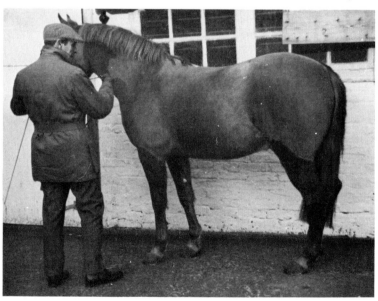

10 The trainer brings the horse to halt

body well in advance of the shoulder, having first moved his whip so that it is held about halfway down its length. The body is then turned inwards towards the horse, the rein hand acts to restrain the movement, the whip is brought up in front of the horse's nose and the command 'Whoah' is given. The horse can then be made to stand up square before being rewarded; we do not want him to stand unevenly with a trailing hindleg. If he is allowed to get into this habit of halting unevenly it will appear again when he is ridden under saddle and will then be far more difficult to eradicate. A halt that is not square means that the horse is unbalanced, and he cannot, therefore, move off smartly into walk since he must first bring up his trailing leg before he can go forward, or, for that matter, and when we reach that point, go backwards in a correct rein-back.

We have to recognize, however, that at this stage the horse is not developed and may experience difficulty in halting squarely. We can help him by asking for the halt on a shallow curve. If, for instance, he continually trails his left hindleg, make a curve to the left which will cause the left hindleg to be engaged further under the body and which should ensure, if we time it correctly, that the leg remains there when the horse is brought to halt.

This work is continued into **Stage 3**, when it can be extended to include the trot in-hand and when we shall endeavour to perfect the move-off and the forward progression, countering any reluctance by the use of the whip. Should the horse stop at any time resist the temptation to move your own body forward: instead retreat a pace, lengthening the rein and applying the whip to make him go forward on to the hand.

During Stages 2 and 3, and in those that follow, it is probably better to alter the routine so that the work period is divided into two sessions of shorter duration. In both sessions a period of concentrated work must be followed by relaxation. Let the horse have a nibble of grass or allow him to watch a tractor at work or to observe, from a safe distance, passing traffic on the roadway.

Always remember to teach the horse to lead in-hand from *both sides*. Since, for most people, it is easier to lead from the nearside, it is as well to devote the first half of the lesson to leading from the offside, otherwise this side is likely to get only five minutes as an afterthought.

The stable training in **Stage 3** is advanced to include the teaching of some simple movements, and we can begin a daily wisping session of twenty minutes or so to tone up the existing muscle and to assist in its further development. We continue to use our weighted sack and in addition we begin to lean our body over the back, if necessary employing an up-turned bucket to help us get into this position.

Using our long whip, with which the horse is now quite familiar, we can practise getting him to stand up square for a few minutes each day, tapping his legs with the whip if necessary so that he places them correctly. We can also teach him to move backwards for just one or two steps. It is very easy to teach this movement in-hand, and if we continue it will stand us in good stead for the future. Place the horse against a wall, standing square, and induce him to lower his head slightly by holding your hand under his nose as though it contained a titbit. Give him the command 'go back' at the same time as your hand passes to his chest to give him a little push. Usually, the horse will take a distinct step back with a foreleg and the opposite hindleg. He can be kept straight by the long whip, held in the other hand, lying along his flank. One step, using either diagonal, is sufficient to start with and the horse should then be encouraged to walk smartly forward and given his reward. If you can obtain, eventually, two distinct steps, without the quarters evading by being swung outwards, that will be quite enough. Should the horse not retreat from a push on the chest, tread on his toe – he will soon get used to the idea.

The daily wisping, using a dampened rope of twisted hay or, if you find it difficult to make, a roughly sewn chamois bag stuffed with hay, has to be done properly if it is to be of any value, and if the animal is not to be scared out of his wits time must be allowed for him to become accustomed to the thumping action of the pad before the latter is applied with the full strength of the arm. After a week or two, however, we should be able to wisp the muscles of the neck, shoulders and quarters standing well back from the horse and delivering rhythmical, sweeping strokes with a reasonable degree of force. Do not, of course use the wisp too near his head, nor in the loin area. The build-up of muscle obtained by this method is quite remarkable, and as our horse gets bigger we shall more easily see in which departments he tends to be deficient and can then devote more attention to these areas.

If it is at all possible we should try to spend no less than one and a quarter hours per day grooming and wisping the horse and hand-rubbing his legs. Hand-rubbing of the legs is a good practice, stimulating the circulation and general tone, as well as providing an excellent opportunity of discovering any slight puffiness or superficial knocks. Rub always towards the heart, locking both hands round the leg and applying pressure on the upward strokes. In general it is best to groom after exercise, when the horse is warm and the skin pores open. Wisping and any other massage techniques are best left to the afternoon or evening for the reason that circulation, which slows down at night, will be stimulated by these practices.

I use a massage technique of my own (described in a previous book of mine, *The Horseman's Guide**) which can be just as profitably carried out with a young horse as with an older one. It does, however (or so I'm now told), require a strength in the fingers which I didn't realize I possessed, and one must exercise care in its application. The first part is easy, and consists of rubbing the whole of the horse's body with the forearms and closed hands. The knack is to move the arms in a small circular motion with the full weight of the body behind the movements. You increase the pressure on that part of the circle nearest the heart and decrease it as the arm is moving away from the heart area. Tight muscles, which you can feel with experience, will soon relax and if the horse could purr, he would. Failing this appreciative accompaniment, mine lower their heads, close their eyes and doze.

The second part takes in the legs below the knees and hocks and commences with an alternate squeezing and releasing of the bulbs of the heels. You then work upwards to the coronary band and pastern using stiffened, probing fingers and a degree of pressure. Next the legs are hand-rubbed, as already described, preferably using an astringent lotion, such as Radiol spirit. This second part is completed by the stretching, backwards and forwards, of each leg. But don't expect to get much movement out of a youngster on the first few occasions; let it come gradually, and under no circumstances force the leg to go further than is obviously comfortable, otherwise you could damage a muscle.

The third and final stage involves the neck, the back muscles and the spine. Starting at the poll, you knead the crest with your fingers, rolling it from side to side, and continue the kneading movement down to the withers. From there on to the croup, the thumbs and the heels of the hand are used to flex the spine. One must, of course, be very careful around the loins but the response made by the horse is quite extraordinary, and there is no surer way of detecting tension or tenderness in the back area which might otherwise go unnoticed.

A last word about handling the horse in the stable before we get onto Stage 4. Please don't treat a young horse or any other as though he were a time-bomb ready to explode at any moment, and don't allow anyone else to either. Approach him confidently, treat him kindly and with firmness and he will respond in the same fashion. Hop about him like an agitated sparrow, squeaking 'whoa boy', and touching him with fluttering hands and the pair of you will be reduced to nervous wrecks in no time at all. Personally, in these early

* Country Life, 1969.

days, I would never allow any stranger, however well intentioned, to approach a young horse of mine in his box. The type to be avoided most assiduously are the bluff hearty chaps who long to tell you tall stories of their exploits in the saddle. Avoid them like the plague; the damage they will do to your youngster in five minutes will take days to put right.

Chapter 8   Phase 1, Stage 4: Lungeing

Whatever progress we have made so far has been very largely to do with the mental outlook of the horse. In Stage 4 we shall still be concerned with his mental development but we shall also be directing our attention to the build-up of his physical condition. To prepare the horse to carry weight on his back we make use of that so frequently misunderstood gymnastic exercise, lungeing.

Lungeing is just as much an art as riding, and is possibly by far the most important aspect in the horse's training; it is, as much as any other exercise, the foundation upon which everything that follows is built. But it must be properly done or so much damage can be caused as to ruin the horse forever.

I once read a book in which the author described lungeing as 'a tedious penance undertaken by only the most dedicated'. That one sentence was enough to make me lose all confidence in whatever else he had to say. I admit that I find lunge work fascinating and entirely absorbing and find it difficult to understand why it should not appear in the same light to others. In fact, I sometimes wonder whether the people who denigrate this favourite exercise of mine neither know what its purpose is, nor appreciate what benefits it incorporates. And if that sounds extraordinarily arrogant it has to be recognized that there *are* some extraordinarily odd ideas held about lungeing and that very few people seem to take the trouble to master the relatively simple techniques involved.

For this reason I am going to define the objectives of the lunge work before explaining the methods by which they can be gained.

First, the **Physical Objectives**, which are:

1   To promote the build-up of muscles without their being formed in opposition to the weight of a rider. Further, to develop those muscles, both those working in opposition and and those working in pairs, equally on either side of the body.

2   To supple the horse laterally by the equal stretching (and, therefore, contraction) of the dorsal, neck and abdominal muscles on either side.

3 To induce tension of the spine by encouraging an extended neck and head carriage and the engagement of the hindlegs. This must always be easier on a circle since the inside leg is bound to be more actively engaged beneath the body.

4 To increase the flexion of the joints, which will occur as a result of greater and more supple muscular development.

5 To flex the spine, as far as this is possible, correcting the natural curvature of the horse.

6 To improve the balance, an objective best achieved on the circle, at this stage, because of the need to engage the hocks.

Then there are the **Mental Objectives**, which are just as important:

1 The inculcation of **Calm**.

2 To accustom the horse to the **Habit** of discipline and to teach him obedience to the first of the aids – the voice.

3 Finally, a most essential consideration, which is both a **Physical** and **Mental** quality – to teach the horse to **Go Forward**.

Additionally, the advanced work on the lunge, which frankly is difficult for all but the skilled exponents, will produce bonuses in the way of longitudinal suppling and placing the horse on the bit.

11 An early lunge lesson

Lungeing Method

Fundamentally, lungeing implies a horse describing a circle round his trainer, the two being connected by a lunge rein from the horse's cavesson to the trainer's hand.

Now, this is a perfectly reasonable definition of the exercise but from the outset let us get rid of the ridiculous idea, propounded by old gentlemen who should know better, that lungeing, to be effective, demands that the horse makes a perfect circle round a trainer who pivots on a fixed heel rammed firmly into the ground.

This is nonsense *as far as the early lessons* of the young horse are concerned and more potentially good animals have been spoilt by adherence to this fallacious ruling than for almost any other reason. In the later stages of training, of course, we require a near-perfect circle with the horse's whole body flexed in the direction of the movement, but this is just too much to ask of a three-year-old and we shall only obtain it for short periods from a four-year-old. To attempt the near-perfect circle in the opening stages of the work is to provoke resistance on the part of the horse because it is asking the impossible of his physical development. Let us by all means bear the ultimate objective of the near-perfect circle in mind but let us, also, appreciate that there are other considerations which must precede this desirable end. Not the least of these is first, to teach the horse what is wanted of him on the lunge. Until he has learnt to go forward and does so in a calm and reasonable manner in both directions we are not going to get a track resembling an Easter egg let alone a circle.

Let us, therefore, study the method to be employed in these first lessons. We shall need an assistant with a lead rein; the horse will wear his cavesson, with the lunge line attached to the centre nose ring, and his boots, whilst the trainer will exchange his training whip for the lunge whip. The training in-hand will, if it has been done thoroughly, be a good preparation for the lunge work, which is, indeed, only an extension of the former.

The lesson is commenced, therefore, by the trainer walking the horse round the manege, practising the transitions upwards and downwards from halt to trot. (An upward transition is from one pace to a faster one, and a downward one an alteration to a slower pace and to halt.). Quite possibly the horse will have already made small circles round his trainer, so as we enter a corner, we can lengthen the rein and walk the horse round in a circle, gradually reducing the circle made by ourselves until we are virtually standing still whilst the horse walks round us. (This is not to be confused with pivoting on the heel.) The horse should now be rewarded, and then the walking exercise commenced again. When the horse walks round the trainer calmly the assistant, with her lead rein attached to a side-ring of the cavesson, can lead the horse, walking at his shoulder on the opposite side to the trainer. That is, if we are circling left, she will be on the offside and vice-versa. The trainer (still, of course, holding the lunge looped in his left hand, if the circle is to the left) will gradually move further away from the horse and position himself in a line slightly to the rear of the horse's hip. In his right hand he carries his lunge whip by the butt, its point on the ground behind him. By making sweeping movements with the whip behind the horse, letting the thong trail along the ground, he can encourage his pupil to keep moving forward. The assistant, who should hold her lead in the lightest contact, can help in this respect if she carries a long whip and uses it in the way described previously.

When this point is reached we can begin teaching our pupil to obey the voice; something which he should not find difficult if we have carried out the training in-hand thoroughly. The actual words we use are unimportant; it is the tone in which they are given that matters. Nevertheless, it is probably wise to stick such words as 'Whoa', 'Walk-on', 'Terrot', 'steady boy', and so on. The cardinal rule to be observed is that those words asking for an increase in pace should end on a sharp, upward note whilst those requesting a slow-down need to be long-drawn out and as soothing as possible. What must be remembered is that these are words of *command* and should be given as such. It is no good whispering 'trot', 'whoa', in the same tone of voice; each command must be quite distinct and distinguishable from any other. This doesn't mean that one shouts – that only upsets the horse – but we must make quite sure that he hears and understands. Later on, when the horse is familiar with the exercise, it will be found that the commands can be given so quietly that someone standing at the other end of the manege will not be able to hear them. But at first, take no chances and speak out bold and clear.

The assistant helps the horse by urging him on or restraining him according to the word of command given. For the first few lessons we concentrate on no more than the halt and the walk-on and we work, of course, to either hand. On the trainer giving the command 'walk-on' he simultaneously uses his whip in a brushing movement along the ground behind the horse and at the same time moves his rein hand slightly towards the direction of the movement. If the horse does not make an immediate response the assistant supports the command by tapping the flank with her long whip. To halt, the word of command is accompanied by a very gentle tensioning of the rein made by little jerks of the fingers which cease the moment the horse obeys. Once again the assistant can help by exerting similar tensions on her lead rein if it is necessary. Once the horse stops, the trainer can approach him and reward him with a pat or even an *occasional* titbit, and he should then ensure that the horse is standing correctly with both fore- and hindfeet in line. If we continually check the halt, right from the beginning, halting correctly will become a habit in the horse.

To change the rein the horse must be brought to halt. The trainer then switches his whip and rein from one hand to the other and takes up his position opposite the horse's hip, whilst the assistant changes over to the opposite side.

The trot will be just as easily taught as the walk-on, although it will require more exertion on the part of the long-suffering assistant.

Once this pace is established, as well as the walk and halt, the assistant can gradually, over a period of possibly three short lessons, reduce her influence until the horse will move round his trainer, and obey him, without her help. At this stage, however, it is more than likely that the horse will try to be disobedient by either turning in towards the trainer or refusing to go forward. The assistant should, therefore, be positioned for at least a few of the following lessons behind the horse, where she can help the trainer to counteract anything of this nature by urging the horse *forward* with threatening movements of her whip.

You will notice that emphasis has been placed on the assistant being always on the outside of the horse and on the trainer walking out to the horse and never allowing his pupil to come into the centre. I am aware that this is not always accepted practice but there are good reasons for it. In the first place, I want the horse's attention devoted entirely to me, and the presence of an assistant between myself and him, as would be the case if she were to lead from the inside, presents a dividing physical barrier which cannot help but detract from this end. Similarly, I do not allow the assistant to reward the horse since I want him to associate that pleasure with the trainer whose commands he obeys. I *never* allow the horse to come into the centre, because once he has learnt to do so and has been encouraged by a reward he will continually turn inwards in the natural hope of receiving the same treatment again. It is much better to halt the horse correctly on the circle and to make him stand immobile whilst one walks quietly up to him. There is, after all, no sense in creating difficulties.

Once the trainer is lungeing the horse on his own he can begin to ask for a more accurate circle and an altogether more active performance at trot, which is the most valuable of the paces on the lunge. Again, however, we must not go too

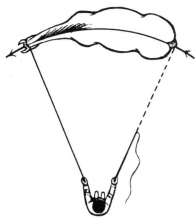

Figure 16
The 'Triangle of control' on the lunge.

quickly nor expect results too soon. The circles must be kept large (too small a circle causes the quarters to be thrown outside the track), the trainer moving initially with the horse in concentric circles and always maintaining what I term the *Triangle of Control*. By this I mean that the trainer, standing on a line just behind the hip represents the apex, the horse itself the base, whilst the whip and rein form the two sides. Always the horse must go forward from the whip into the hand, just as later he will move forward into the bit in response to the rider's legs. (See Figure 16.)

After a dozen lessons or so, however, it should be possible to obtain good circles for very short periods, with the horse moving forward fairly rhythmically, the hindlegs tracking the forefeet, and with the head bent in the direction of the movement. This latter can be encouraged by the trainer exerting intermittent pressures on the rein by the opening and closing of the fingers with the hand held on a level with the cavesson. These first lessons on the lunge should not exceed fifteen minutes or so and should be punctuated with rest periods during which our old friend, the weighted sack, can be placed over the horse's back whilst he investigates a small bowl of oats.

Once again it is wise to start the lessons on the right rein, which is the most difficult, usually, for both horse and trainer. It is always a temptation to go on working to the left because it is easier, and then to find that only a couple of minutes remain in which to work to the opposite direction. If we always start to the right we shall ensure that the muscles concerned get their fair share of the work and we shall avoid producing a one-sided horse.

12 and *13* During a lunge lesson the horse has attempted to spin round, and the trainer quickly counteracts this disobedience

We shall be lucky, however, if we do not meet with some little resistance during this period, and it is as well to be fore-warned of the evasions which are likely to arise. Quite frequently, and quite illogically, horses will resent changing the rein and will run back as the trainer attempts to move round their front to the opposite side. The answer is to perform the movement slowly, talking quietly all the time, and, once having got to the opposite side, to run one's hand down the neck, working towards the shoulder and then the flank, before moving outwards. Even when the horse has been got going in the required direction he may still try to turn round. Fortunately, he will make, almost invariably, an inward turn. We must then move quickly to get behind the horse, using our whip vigorously (but on the ground, not lifted in the air) to make him move forward. We must not hit the horse but it may be that the consequence of our action will be to cause him to bound forward suddenly, and so we must be ready to give with our rein. He is, after all, only obeying us, and he must not be discouraged by getting a bump on the nose – that would only confuse him and make him less inclined to obey us next time. Should he attempt to take-off we must again be sympathetic in our actions whilst remaining firmly in control. There is no point in starting a tug-of-war, which may result in our being dragged along, literally *ventre à terre*, behind a terrified horse, so we must go with him as best we can, restraining him gradually by a series of sharp little tugs on the rein until he quietens down and circles us once more. It may be possible to stop a small three-year-old by force, for a cavesson is a fairly powerful instrument, but it is more than probable that the horse will be spun round on his forelegs. And that is the best way of causing strains and sprains that I know.

14 This small pony has halted abso-lutely square and stands listening for the next command

Occasionally, particularly when the horse is fresh, he may refuse to slow down or come to halt and we should not let this worry us too much. If he should disregard the voice, a little flip on the lunge rein, causing a ripple down its length, which finishes up with a smack on the nose will often be enough to make him pay attention. However, if this fails, encourage him to go just a little faster and when he shows signs of wanting to slow up persist in sending him on for a moment or two before asking him to halt. He will then be ready enough to do so. Where the horse is really naughty we can have recourse to the wall of the manege or the corner. It is quite simple to drive him into the wall, when he must, willy nilly, come to a halt. This is effective but should not be practised except in the last resort. It is far better to avoid trouble of this kind by not asking for the halt until the horse has settled down and one senses that he is ready to obey. The only way to get a horse to relax is to relax physically and mentally yourself. If you become irritated by the horse's behaviour, and show it by becoming tense, things will only go from bad to worse.

Two difficulties can arise from working on the circle. Either the horse can pull against the rein or he can fall in towards the centre. In the first instance he is usually pulling away because he finds the circle too tight for comfort. The solution is to make it larger and so remove the cause of the evasion. Falling in is a way of escaping the effort involved in bending the body on the circle and is combated by pointing the whip, held fairly low again, at the offending shoulder.

We can also expect the horse to be a bit lazy sometimes, doing just as little as he thinks he can get away with safely. In essence he is not moving forward, or at any rate the forward urge is not sufficiently evident, and he must, therefore, be urged on by the trainer moving a pace or two to the rear of the line with the hip in order to get behind his pupil.

Then, of course, most young horses will indulge in a buck or two. Usually this is nothing more than high spirits and is best ignored. But if the horse persists in bucking beyond a reasonable limit he must be brought to order by a sharp flip on the lunge to remind him of his manners.

Finally, there are just one or two characters who may be bold enough to come into the centre and at the trainer, looking as though they intended tearing him limb from limb. Fortunately, they are seldom encountered, but if you have one who behaves in this fashion he must be dealt with very firmly. The secret again is to get to one side of him and slightly to the rear so that he can be driven forward. One must, however, move towards him swiftly and resolutely to show him that, far from being frightened, the boot is on the other foot and that the subject of his attack is well prepared to retaliate. Strangely

15 Miss Sylvia Stanier working a young horse

enough, horses of this type often turn out the best in the end, once they have submitted to discipline. One experienced trainer used to say that he liked a horse who put up a fight early on and got it out of his system rather than one who saved it up for when a rider was on his back. There is some truth in this but, in general, fights are not often necessary and we can usually get our way without descending to a brawl.

The Roller

Whilst the work in the stable described in the previous stage continues, it is now necessary to get the horse to accept the roller, for which he has been prepared by the weighted sack. Any new experience should, of course, be left until after the horse has worked, and this one is no exception.

Leave the roller on the manger during grooming periods for a day or two and let the horse sniff it and touch it with his nose. Nine out of ten will take no notice of it at all, but it is as well to be sure. Similarly, the horse is unlikely to resent the roller being put on his back on top of a soft pad; he may, however, become worried when it is fastened round his belly. To avoid trouble resist the temptation to fasten up the roller immediately; instead, place one hand on the top of the roller pad and with the other pull the loose end towards you so that pressure is put on the animal's girth. Do this for half-a-dozen times, if necessary, do it for two or three days, until the horse will accept the pressure quite happily and the roller can be fastened up gently but not too tightly. So far so good, but any squalls that are likely to blow up will occur when the horse feels the friction of the roller as he moves and hears the little squeak that leather usually makes. We can give the horse some idea of what to expect by walking him round his box as we have done so often before. He may give a little hump or two, but if after a few circuits his feed is brought in and he is allowed to get his nose into the manger his oats will help him to forget the slight discomfort he experiences.

Initally, when the horse is lunged in the roller there is a possibility that he will be reluctant to move forward as freely as before, and it will be necessary to bear this in mind and to act accordingly with quiet firmness.

From now on he will always work in his roller, and it is a good idea to leave the article in place for an hour or two each day in the stable. It will help to harden up his skin. In fact, to assist the hardening process it is of benefit to give daily applications of surgical spirit to those parts with which the roller comes into contact. We should, of course, pay particular attention to the girth area, especially round the elbows, at our daily inspection. In this respect, whilst it would be stupid to adjust the roller so tight as to cut the horse in two, we should avoid the opposite extreme of fastening it so loosely as to allow it to slip forward on to the soft skin wrinkles immediately behind the elbows. To prevent this happening and to avoid fastening the roller too tightly many people advocate the use of a crupper, which will certainly achieve these two objects and is helpful with a young horse whose front-end is as yet lacking in development. However, if a crupper is worn it must be adjusted most carefully and, of course, be exceptionally soft and well padded round the dock. The danger that can accompany its use is that the horse will resist the unaccustomed pressure on his tail and hollow his back as a result – something we just do not wish to encourage. In any case, a horse will usually buck, with a tail clamped between his buttocks, when he is first lunged in a crupper. Usually this is no more than a passing phase but it can be pretty violent while it lasts and we should be prepared for a few minor fireworks.

Other Activities

To vary the work on the lunge we can use a part of the exercise period very profitably by taking the horse for quiet walks, during which he can have a look at some traffic. A good place from which he can view traffic safely is at that sort of road junction which has a convenient square of grass on one side or the other. He can be allowed to nibble away whilst the traffic passes by and on the first few occasions it will be helpful if he is accompanied by an older steady horse.

It is obviously not very sensible to take the youngster into heavy traffic at this stage. But there is no reason why he should not get used to a Land Rover being driven about quietly near the training area and to watch and listen to such things as a domestic lawnmower in action. If he shows fright, however, do not persist but instead introduce the object to him gradually, even to the extent of feeding him off the bonnet, if it is a car or a Land Rover, until he will feed with equanimity whilst the engine is running. Make use, too, of the older horse who will be able to set an example for the youngster and whose presence will calm his quite natural apprehension. In addition, even as early in the training as this, get the horse used to water. You can start by running the hosepipe on the ground immediately round him until he is standing in a puddle and progress to the point where he will allow the water to be played over his legs. On your walks make use of the countryside, leading the horse over little banks and ditches and generally teaching him to look after himself. Seize every opportunity to walk through streams but do remember your gumboots, it is you who will have to go in first!

In the schooling area put the odd sack over the rails, shifting it about each day and place something like an old chair just outside the rails, shifting its position as with the sacks. Then don't forget the radio. It is just as valuable to have it blaring away round the training ground as in the vicinity of the stable.

Shoes

With the horse beginning to get into regular work shoes will be necessary to avoid any foot soreness. If our preparation has been thorough the fitting of his first set of shoes should cause no trouble, but do give the horse time to get used to the feel of them. To start with, the weight on his feet will bother him a little and it will certainly affect his action for a short time. Recognize that this is so and don't ask too much of him for a day or two. Anyone who has seen an intake of raw recruits into a regiment of the old Indian Army will testify how clumsily these young lads walked when first fitted out with boots, after having gone virtually barefoot for most of their lives. The young horse is in much the same position.

Chapter 9

Phase 1, Stage 5: Introduction to Bit and Saddle

This stage is concerned first with the introduction of the bit into the horse's mouth and subsequently with getting him to *accept* the bit, which is a very different thing to shoving one between his jaws. Secondly, which is complementary to the aim of obtaining acceptance, is the encouragement of the correct rounded form in movement. In itself, this rounded form, with the consequent strengthening of the back it will induce, is a preparation for carrying weight. Lastly, in this stage, we will get the horse used to working with a saddle on his back.

The Bit

Putting a bit into the mouth of a young horse is frequently a rather terrifying operation for both parties. But it needn't be, nor should we imagine that it will present any difficulty. After all, our horse is well used to our handling his mouth, we have been doing it regularly every day, and by this time he should have no fear of having his ears touched.

The first step is to fasten the bit of our choice on to the *offside* of the cavesson by means of either a bit clip or a small strap, having first made sure that the nose of the cavesson is not fastened tightly. To make the exercise a pleasurable experience we can smear the bit with treacle, which is messy, or we can wrap it with a small bandage enclosing layers of sugar. This, however, will mean the end of the bandage. It is probably easier to cut some thin slices of carrot and hold both them and the bit in your hand. The bit and carrot slice are then passed quietly into the mouth and the former secured on the near-side. Having got the bit in leave it in place for an hour or so each day and work the horse with the bit just hanging in his mouth – no side-reins yet!

In the stable the horse can be given a small feed whilst he is wearing the bit. In this way he learns the first 'mouthing' lesson, being compelled in the act of mastication to relax his lower jaw. I am not in favour of leaving the bit in the mouth for extended periods as the practice can encourage the horse in bad habits. Left alone in his stable for hours on end he can too easily begin to experiment with the piece of metal in his mouth; twisting it this way and that and possibly learning how to set his jaw against it, or even how to push his tongue over the top.

One must, of course, be very careful that the bit is properly fitted in the mouth and is of the correct width. Ideally the ends of the mouthpiece should project about half-an-inch on either side of the mouth and it should be adjusted just high enough to cause a tiny wrinkle in the lips, almost as though the horse was smiling. Too narrow a mouthpiece causes discomfort and resistance; too large a bit encourages the horse to slide the bit through his mouth and so evade its proper action; a bit fixed too high is uncomfortable and one placed too low may bang the teeth and is a positive encouragement of the vice of placing the tongue over the bit, an action which entirely defeats the latter's purpose.

From here it is a comparatively simple business to put on a complete bridle but the job should be tackled in easy stages. Bridling is not a very comfortable experience for some horses who will regularly have their teeth banged and their ears pulled about in the process. We don't want any of that sort of trouble with our youngster, so to start with it is best to dispense with browband and noseband, introducing them only when he allows the headpiece to be slipped over his ears without difficulty. The noseband is not really a problem but it does get in the way sometimes. In any case we shall not need it for the moment as the bridle will be worn under the cavesson for some little time yet.

Lungeing – Seeking the Bit

Our object now is to cause the horse to reach forward to make contact with his bit, in fact 'to seek it out' at all times.

To this end the side-reins will in due course be brought into use, but they must be employed carefully and the trainer should be quite certain in his own mind what it is he is trying to obtain. Generally speaking, the whole concept of side-reins, or rather the use of them, is much misunderstood. A lot is said, and indeed written, about 'pulling the horse together,' implying a continual shortening of the side-reins from the moment they are first used. Employed in this way the side-reins impose a head-carriage, a subject with which adherents of this school seem to be obsessed. What does not appear to be recognized is that the young horse's balance and particularly his muscular development is not yet ready or able to produce the sort of high head-carriage that these people want, and try to obtain too quickly by force.

Muscles can only contract naturally and easily to the extent to which they can be stretched. Any contraction forced upon them before they have been made to stretch must necessarily be forced and will therefore produce resistance and an incorrect head-carriage, usually accompanied by the neck 'caving in' in front of the withers. Furthermore, tight side-reins at this point will result in a false 'withdrawal' of the head. The horse, far from accepting the bit, gets his mouth behind it and out of contact. With the neck and head in that position there can be no tension of the back with the consequent rounding of the top line and the engagement of the hindlegs. The horse then moves with a hollow back and trailing hindlegs.

As I see it, the side-reins have two functions, both of which *contribute* to the formation of a good head carriage. I use the word contribute deliberately, since the origin of the higher head-carriage is the result of greater engagement of the hocks. This results in a shift of weight towards the quarters, and a subsequent lightening and raising of the forehand and of the agents of balance – the head and neck. The first function of the side-rein is to assist the horse to make contact with his bit and at the same time encourage the rounded back and engaged hindlegs which will ultimately result in the head being raised naturally.

Initially, therefore, the side-reins must be *long* and be increased in length rather than shortened to encourage the essential dropping and stretching of the neck and head reaching for contact with the bit – a process which, by the cervical ligament being stretched over the fulcrum of the withers, tensions the back.

Later in the training, when we have obtained a good engagement behind, and the head and neck are raised naturally, we can assist the horse to find an even better and steady carriage of the head by shortening the side-reins correspondingly. The neck muscles having already been stretched are then ready to accept compression, but not before. If the first steps are omitted and the side-reins shortened up immediately we will spoil our horse for the reasons given.

I am well aware that a great many people disregard this first function of the side-reins but no *logical* argument is ever advanced to support the practice. I do not deny that *a* result can be achieved, but I do assert that it is an incorrect one and that the horses concerned would probably have been better off if no side-reins had been used at all. Watch any average class of show-ponies – very few of them move from behind, however extravagantly they point their toe in front.

The Lunge Work

In the first lessons that are given when the horse is wearing his bit no side-reins are needed. We are giving him time to get used to the feel of the bit, and in any case we need to concentrate on obtaining the correct form in movement *before* we start meddling with the mouth.

So far, our horse has learnt to obey our voice and we should have succeeded in getting him to work on the lunge at trot on a fairly good circle. His head will be carried naturally and rather low and there should be a noticeable bend of the body in the direction of the movement with an increasing engagement of the hindlegs. Now we need to carry this a stage further and encourage a better rhythm, greater engagement of the hocks and a more noticeable stretching of head and neck forwards and downwards. These last two requirements will contribute to an improvement in the top line.

We shall be helped in these respects by the use of stout poles laid on the ground which the horse will be asked to cross over. The first exercise involves the use of just a single pole laid on the track. Over this our horse must be taught to move, first at walk and then at trot without making a jump. It may be necessary to lead him over the pole at first if he seems inclined to rush. Under no circumstances should he trot over the pole until he crosses over it at the walk quite calmly. Inevitably, as the horse approaches the pole, he will extend his neck and lower his head, which is just what we want, but we must not allow the rhythm to be lost.

16 Walking over poles on the ground

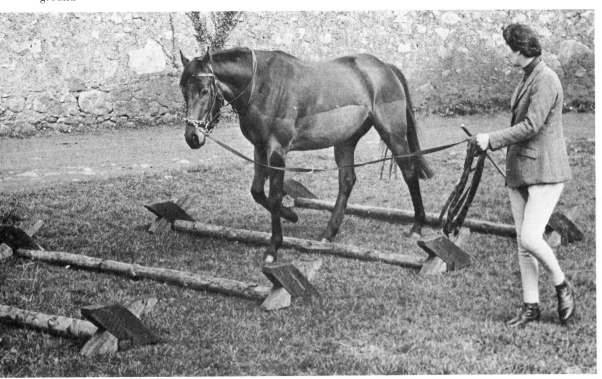

Within the space of two lessons another pole can be introduced on the opposite side of the circle and within a short
while the horse will be trotting happily over both, rounding
his back as he does so.

The next step is to make a grid of three, and then four, poles
laid in a straight line and spaced between 5 and 6 feet apart,
depending on the horse's stride at trot. Watch this distance
carefully, shortening or lengthening it as seems necessary for
the individual concerned. For the horse to progress over this
grid he must be allowed to make a straight approach and to
continue for a few yards on the same straight line after passing
over the last pole. Later on, much later on, these poles may
be placed in a circle, but at this stage our horse is not sufficiently balanced to attempt this more advanced exercise with
any hope of performing it with advantage.

17 The same exercise at trot

The grid will accentuate the engagement of the hocks and
the general rounding of the form and as such it is an excellent
strengthening and suppling exercise. In addition it serves
two other most important purposes. In the first place, the
stretching forward of the head with nose as the foremost part
of the progression is a preparation for his reaching forward to
seek the bit and an essential element in placing him '*on* the bit'
later in the training. Secondly, the crossing of these poles is in
reality his first introduction to jumping. As the horse becomes
more proficient at the exercises we shall increase his activity by
raising the poles up to six inches from the ground. In the
following stages we will obtain the maximum benefit from the
exercise by substituting cavalletti for the poles.

Having got our work over the grid pretty well established we
can return to the mouth and those side-reins.

Before using the side-reins, however, the horse must become accustomed to the slight weight of a rein on his mouth. For this purpose we can use an ordinary rein fastened to the bit rings and secured to the centre dee of the roller, at the buckle end. The rein will then hang loosely imposing no tension on the mouth. The next step is to fit the side-reins from middle dees on either side of the roller pads to the rear rings on the cavesson, not to the bit rings. The side-reins should be adjusted almost at their full length so that a light pressure is felt on the nose only when the head and neck are stretched out almost to their full extent.

Before working the horse in this tackle spend some ten minutes on the grid, approaching it, of course, on both reins, to get the horse reaching forward. Then fit the side-reins and work on the ordinary circle trying to push the horse into taking up the slack of the side-rein, by sending him up from the whip hand. This will take a few days to accomplish, and I find a result can be obtained more effectively if I tighten up the side-reins for a few moments, working the horse on the shortened reins for three or four circles to either hand. On lengthening the side-reins again the horse will almost always react by reaching forward into contact with them with increased vigour. One must be careful, however, not to allow the slightest retraction of the nose towards the chest. This is an evasion of the pressure which, if persisted in, leads to the 'overbent' horse, the horse who is 'behind his bit', instead of in contact with it and his rider's hand, and a horse who is consequently not under control. Usually a retraction is made because the reins are too tight, and the solution is to lengthen them right out again and defer any further shortening for a day or two. (See Figures 17a–17d.)

It must be remembered that whenever we use side-reins the adjustment will vary according to the pace at which the horse is working. The correct tension for trot, which is the pace most valuable for lungeing or schooling work since it is possible to work all the muscles more effectively, is not correct for either walk or canter. The walk need hardly concern us, but in later stages we shall do some work at canter and will then have to lengthen the reins to accommodate this movement.

There is a school of thought which recommends that the side-reins should be adjusted more tightly on the inside and correspondingly lengthened on the outside to allow for the bend of head and neck. My personal opinion is that this practice is more likely to be harmful than beneficial, and I adjust my side-reins exactly equal on both sides. The disadvantages of the shorter-on-the-inside system are that the enforced, and frequently exaggerated, bend can cause the horse either to hang on to the inside of his bit or to retract his nose to avoid its contact. Additionally, in resistance he bends his neck some-

Figure 17a
The horse stretching his neck when working on long side-reins so as to 'seek out' contact with the bit. The rounded top line remains in evidence.

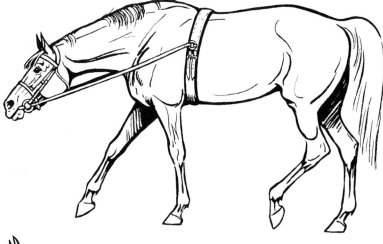

Figure 17b
As the balance improves, the side-reins are shortened to encourage a higher head carriage.

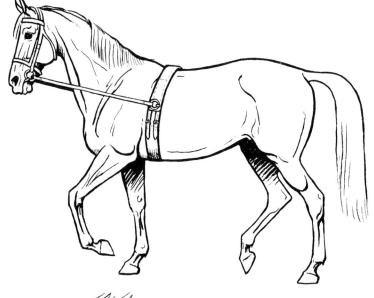

Figure 17c
The horse may evade the bit by 'over-bending' if the side-reins are adjusted too tightly, too soon. The horse's mouth is then 'behind' the bit.

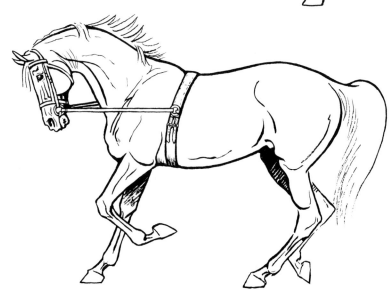

Figure 17d
Another form of evasion produced by incorrect use of the side-reins. The horse is now 'above the bit'. His neck, in front of the withers, and his back are hollowed, and in this position there can be no engagement of the hindlegs.

where around the two-thirds down mark instead of making a slight bend from the poll back. Adherents of the system will argue that it 'supples' the neck, but I am not quite sure what they mean by this. The neck of the horse is already very supple – why to we want to make it more so? Surely, what we should aim for is a build-up of muscles on the top line from poll to withers so that the neck assumes the quality of a tempered steel sword. We require the neck to be as much 'framed' between the reins as the quarters are enclosed between our two legs.

The last thing we want is a twisty, snakey, 'rubber' neck and that I believe is what the unequal side-rein produces. Additionally, this concentration on the bend of the neck can cause us to disregard the *essential* bend which should be from poll to tail. A neck forcibly bent to one side in the majority of instances make a bend throughout the body impossible. Instead the horse swings out the quarters, since there is little else he can do to avoid the discomfort, and is thereby taught to carry his hindlegs outside the track made by the forefeet – an unstraight horse, in fact. Finally, of course, the side-reins should not be fitted when grid work is being done. Occasionally, a skilled trainer may use them at full length over poles on the ground, but unless one is in this category it is better for the less accomplished not to attempt this exercise.

The next step is to remove the ordinary rein and fit the side-reins directly to the bit, proceeding as before until the horse is moving forward in rounded form and in contact with the bit. That is as far as we need go at this stage.

Bit Pressures

We can, however, prepare the ground for teaching the ridden hand aids by spending a few moments each day in the stable accustoming the horse to the various bit pressures. We can start by standing in front of the horse holding a bit ring in either hand and vibrating the bit slightly upwards and to the rear. The horse will respond by momentary relaxations of his lower jaw, and the moment he does so we should discontinue the pressure and reward him. We can also apply a similar pressure on each bit ring separately causing him to drop his nose and relax one side of his jaw accordingly. When he has learnt these little lessons we may take them a stage further in the school just before we finish the work for the day and return him to his stable.

Here the trainer will take up a position on one or other side of the horse a little in advance of the shoulder, holding a die-rein in either hand about 10 inches from the bit. The horse is then persuaded to walk forward and the trainer gives the command 'whoa', followed immediately by the slight vibrations on the reins. These are best applied alternatively rather than simultaneously in this instance, since the latter use of the hands presents no fixed base against which the horse can resist, the pressure being continually shifted from one side to the other. The directional use of the rein can be taught by the vibration of one hand, that nearest to the trainer, coupled with a shift of the hand outwards, causing the horse to make a shallower turn. A few minutes each day is quite sufficient, and the trainer must be at pains to reward the horse immediately he drops his nose and relaxes the lower jaw in response to the rein action.

Saddling Procedure

The last object in this Stage is to get the horse to accept a saddle on his back.

As usual we start in the stable, placing the saddle in the manger for a day or two to allow the horse to sniff and touch it.

There are some terrible tales told of the first attempts to put on a saddle, but if a logical progression has been followed, each action being a preparation for the one which is to follow, there is no reason why the horse should not submit to the new experience with equanimity. In our progression we have already worked up to placing a weighted sack on the back each day and the horse is well used to wearing a roller; a saddle, therefore, is not going to be very much of a surprise to him. However, we will take nothing for granted. We do not want to give the horse any reason or opportunity for playing up.

The first attempt to put the saddle on will be made after the exercise period when the horse has got any itch out of his heels. Following the same procedure employed with the weighted sack, the assistant stands at the horse's head and feeds him a small bowl of oats. The trainer then takes the saddle (less its irons and girths, but fitted with the sheepskin), places it quietly over the wither and slides it back into position, keeping one hand on it to save it from falling off should the horse make a sudden movement. The saddle can be left in this position for some ten minutes whilst both trainer and assistant make much of the horse, handling him, adjusting the headcollar and so on. This little exercise can be carried out twice daily for two or three days, or until such time as the horse takes no notice at all of the new piece of equipment on his back.

The girth can then be fitted and, as a precaution against the flaps banging up and down when the horse is in movement, a piece of binder twine can be passed over the top of the saddle, through the stirrup leather loops (if these are conveniently placed) and secured under the belly. Now walk the horse round the box as before, urging him forward firmly if he shows any inclination to stop and hump his back.

Any trouble that is going to arise will occur when the horse starts working at trot on the lunge when first wearing his saddle. It is not the weight that worries him but the noise made by the creaking of the leather and the movement of the flaps. We can get over the flap problem, in part, with the piece of binder twine but the creak we can do nothing about – it is something that the horse must learn to accept as common-place.

Nevertheless, it is prudent to take every precaution the first time we plan to lunge in the saddle and to work the horse for some twenty minutes in his usual tackle of cavesson, bit, side-reins and roller *before* changing to the saddle. The side-reins, depending on the pattern used, can be fitted either round the girth strap or clipped to a girth buckle, but it is important that both should be level.

With a modicum of work under his belt the horse is unlikely to make more than a few half-hearted bucks, which can be ignored. But don't count on it – he may just as easily object more violently. If this appears likely, have the assistant lead him on the offside and, after a few circles at walk and one or two at a calm trot, finish for the day, continuing to make use of the assistant on future occasions until the horse comes to accept his saddle.

The next step is to add the leathers and irons, which again

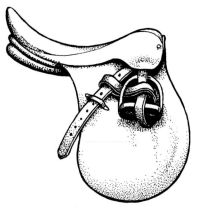

Figure 18
A method of securing the irons and leathers to prevent their swinging when the horse is lunged wearing his saddle.

should be taken at the end of the lesson. These additions *are* going to move about, but the effect can be made less unnerving to the horse if the irons are, at first, run up the leathers and tied together over the top of the saddle with the usual piece of binder twine. The same useful material can be employed to tie the leathers together under the belly, and the binder twine which previously secured the flaps can now be removed. Finally, the irons can be left in their normal position and tied together by twine passing under the belly. This will not immobilize the movement of the irons but it will prevent their swinging about unduly. Incidentally, make sure that the leathers are fairly short so that the tread of the iron does not hang more than a couple of inches below the flap. It is difficult for a horse to cow-kick at the iron and get his foot caught in it but it is not impossible and it has happened with disastrous results.

If every chapter in this book were to finish with a few lines under the heading **Warning – Danger**, the subject for this one would be the side-reins. Use them carefully and, above all, with intelligence.

Chapter 10   Phase 1, Stage 6: Backing

The actual backing operation is usually regarded as the crisis point in the early education largely because the human regards it in this light and so it becomes exaggerated out of its true proportion. In reality there is little more difficulty in putting up a rider than in any other operation in the progression of training. It is certainly far less troublesome than the first few lessons on the lunge. Perhaps the most common mistake is for the trainer to say to himself 'Today, I will back the young horse', and to be determined to carry out his intention come what may. As a result tension is built up, either consciously or otherwise, in the trainer and his assistant and is inevitably passed on to the horse.

The knack lies in knowing when the horse *is ready to be backed*. Naturally, we must make it as easy for the horse as we can by preparing him thoroughly, but it is dangerous to set a time limit on the ultimate conclusion of the exercise.

We may get very near to the point where the rider can at last slip his leg over and sit on the back, but if the horse is not 100 per cent relaxed it is better to postpone the mounting until another day. A sensitive trainer – and by this time all but the most insensitive will have developed some sort of instinctive feeling about their pupil – will know when the moment is ripe and will seize the opportunity.

The preparation for mounting takes place in the stable after work and is more easily accomplished if a bale of straw is handy. Young, supple assistants are well able to vault on to a horse's back but the procedure involves quick and sudden movement which is likely to startle the animal, so for the moment it is best to discard such athletic exercises.

For a day or two the horse can be positioned alongside the bale whilst being groomed; the assistant working up to standing on the bale and rubbing away at the horse's back until she can lie over it and make much of the horse on the opposite shoulder and flank. The trainer, meanwhile, works on the other side, making much of the horse and being ready to deal with any untoward movement. This can be carried out from both sides since this horse is not going to be allowed to develop any one-sided attitudes, whether physical or otherwise.

When the horse allows the assistant to put her full weight over the back the same can be done with the saddle in position until she can put her weight on the iron whilst the trainer exerts an equal downward pressure on the one on the opposite side. The bale can then be moved to the schooling area and each day after the lunge work, whilst the horse is being given a small bowl of oats, the mounting preliminaries can be continued. When the horse is quite relaxed the trainer can give the word to mount and the assistant will quietly, but decisively, put her leg over the horse, making sure it is well clear of the croup as she passes it over the back. She lowers herself gently into the saddle and remains there with the body inclined forward. Immediately she is settled the horse is led forward whilst she makes much of him. Just a few strides is sufficient and then she can dismount, the horse being then rewarded and returned to his stable. Thereafter, the number of strides taken can be increased each day and the rider can gradually sit up straight in the saddle. The reason for holding the body inclined forward is to prevent the horse becoming suddenly alarmed by catching a glimpse (which he is well able to do) of something high up in the air sitting on top of him.

18 Rider mounted, but no loss of calm and no fireworks

If it is thought necessary, a neckstrap may be put on during the first stages, but really a handful of mane is just as effective. It can be useful to have an old horse ridden in the schooling area and being constantly mounted and dismounted in front of the young horse, but, of course, it requires a third person, and if one is not available, we shall probably manage just as well without.

For a week or more the mounted work will be confined to the trainer leading the horse at walk for a few circuits of the arena just before he is returned to the stable. The rider, for her peace of mind, can be provided with a rein attached to the cavesson but will hold it with only the lightest tension. Otherwise she sits still and beyond bringing her legs into light contact with the horse's sides, makes no further movement with them. As the days go on the mounted work takes up an even greater portion of the work periods, but lungeing, carrying out the work already described, still remains an important part and precedes each mounted period.

From walking in-hand to walking and then trotting in *large* circles on the lunge with the rider up will present no problem unless it is that of being tempted to go too fast.

Our objective now is to allow the horse time to become accustomed to carrying weight and to begin to adjust his balance accordingly. The rider may now take up contact on her cavesson reins but as yet there is no need for her to do anything but sit still and go with the movement of the horse. At no time will she *sit* at the trot as this would only cause the horse's back to hollow at this stage.

Trailer Drill

Here we can say the actual backing stage is complete, but there are other aspects of the training which are carried on in conjunction with the work described in Stages 5 and 6. The principal extra-manege training is concerned with boxing drill. Our horse may, in fact, have been boxed as a youngster, but, even so, no harm will be done if this drill is consolidated. Nothing is more infuriating than a horse who will not enter a trailer or box, and in nine cases out of ten it is all for the want of a little intelligent training.

The great prerequisite for trailer-training is discipline, not, unfortunately, a popular word in our day and age but in the training of horses it is necessary. We may live in a permissive society but there is no reason for it to be extended to include our horses. By discipline I do not mean loud voices backed up by whips and a general attitude of 'you'll do as you're told, because I say so'. Far from it: discipline is based upon trust and respect from both parties. We want our horse to know that we will never treat him unfairly and will never ask of him something that is beyond his capacity. When we have achieved that he will obey our requests willingly. Right at the very beginning I stressed the importance of the disciplined horse, and if we have been careful to 'explain' to the horse what we want of him at each stage our training will now stand us in good stead.

In particular, we spent a lot of time teaching him to go forward freely when led in-hand, and by this time it should have become a matter of second nature to him. In theory, therefore, he should walk up the ramp as easily as he submits to being led to and from his stable. In practice, however, this is yet another thing which should not be taken for granted. We do not wish to provoke a trial of strength in which the horse will learn that he is able, even though temporarily, to frustrate our will.

Commence the training by placing the trailer against a wall so that at least one 'wing' is provided and fifty per cent of the danger of running out is at once overcome. Make sure that the ramp is firm and that neither it nor the trailer itself is prone to wobble; nothing upsets a horse so much as an insecure footing. Do also park the trailer with the ramp towards the sun, otherwise the inside will resemble a dark cavern into which few horses will want to venture. Have a feed bowl placed half-way up the ramp on the wall side and then walk the horse on a circle right if it is the right side of the trailer that is against the wall, and vice-versa if it is the opposite way round. Circle the horse close to the ramp so that he can see both it and the food bowl. Now halt him at the ramp and let him inspect it – which he will do in cursory fashion since he will be far more interested in the food – then walk him on again. Make one circuit and again stop at the ramp with the horse on the track of the circle and facing the ramp, therefore, at a slightly oblique angle. If you now step on to the ramp the horse will usually follow and get his nose into the bowl. You can now sit down and occasionally push the bowl a bit further towards the entrance to the trailer, which will make the horse advance at least one leg in order to continue eating. That is the end of the first lesson, and the same procedure will be carried out daily for the next two or even three days. After all, there is no hurry.

When the horse is quite relaxed and evinces an interest in the trailer, which he now associates with food, we can make the actual entry. Circle the horse as before, but instead of putting the feed bowl on the ramp, hold it in your free hand. Make your approach off the circle at a good sharp pace so that the horse strikes the ramp at a slight angle (which makes a run-out more difficult for him) and walk straight in. Reward the horse with the contents of the feed bowl and spend ten minutes or so making much of him. Then take him out. If he has to back out this should not be a problem, as we have taught him how to move back in the box, but have an assistant ready to put a hand on his quarters as he negotiates the ramp, and do not let him hurry. He must move back as he has been taught, under discipline and one step at a time.

Continue to feed the horse in the box but reduce the feed until the reward is no more than a nut or a lump of sugar. When he enters the box easily and we have practised putting the ramp up, move the trailer into different positions until you can load and unload in the middle of the yard. It is well worth taking time over this training to ensure that the exercise becomes an accepted routine.

Finally, we must take the horse for a few short rides, getting the assistant to travel with him for the first few times and driving with the greatest care. Even one bad ride is enough to put a horse off for a considerable period. These rides can be given a purpose, over and above the primary one, by driving to some particular destination, unboxing and then doing a little work (just a walk round is sufficient) before loading up again and returning home. Do, however, remember to take a bowl of oats with you, they may just be needed.

A lunge-rein secured to a point on the trailer and passed round the horse's quarters by an assistant is frequently used when teaching a horse to enter a trailer. The use of a rein in this way is perfectly acceptable but it presupposes that there will always be two people available. What do you do when there is only one?

To conclude this chapter let me stress again the importance of **Daily Examination** of our pupil. Go over his legs most carefully, keeping a watchful eye for any damage, however slight, or any signs of puffiness, and spend a few minutes each day consciously observing his action. If he appears to be a little stiff or to be going rather less freely, stop the work for a couple of days until he is back in form. Also, do not neglect to carry out regular and minute examinations of the mouth. There is no point in exacerbating an inflamed condition caused by teeth-cutting and it is better to remove the bit for a day or two lest the horse should be forced into bad habits.

Secondly, a warning about the use of the lunge. The lunge-ing exercises are some of the most valuable weapons in the trainer's armoury but they are only as good as the man or woman on the end of the lunge rein. Carried out by inexpert hands the exercises can ruin a young horse's action before he ever comes to carrying a rider. Usually the fault lies in working for too long periods and an insistence on tight circles. The first causes the horse's muscles to be over-strained, and inevitably he will work out some way of avoiding the discomfort he is experiencing. We shall then find that he is using his body to oppose the correct bend and form, and if this continues it very quickly becomes an established way of movement.

The second, the tight circles, not only cause a young horse muscular discomfort, to which he will respond as before by making a resistance, but may also cause a shortening of the stride which, once it occurs, will continue throughout the horse's life.

From the viewpoint of the horse's mental development we must appreciate that the work imposes a considerable burden on his limited mind. It is just as possible to overdo his mental capacity as to over-stretch his physical structure, and the results will be just as damaging in both the short and long term. To counteract any possibility of mental fatigue we should make sure that the pupil is given an opportunity to unwind by being allowed the hour or two each day at liberty in his paddock.

No specific time can be put on the work involved up to Stage 6 but normally one would expect to have got this far in three to three and a half months. At the end of this stage our horse should be ready physically to carry weight, although he has, in fact, still to learn *how* to carry it, and he will have taken the first steps towards acceptance of the bit.

In the following stages which complete Phase 1 we shall extend his education to the point where he has learnt to adjust his balance in accordance with the rider's weight and to obey the simple commands made by the rider's aids.

Chapter 11

Phase 1, Stage 7: The Elementary Exercises under Saddle

This is the final stage in the primary education of the three-year-old and, before commencing it, we should again make an appreciation of the objectives which are involved.

1 The horse must be taught to adjust and improve his balance under the weight of the rider. Having *accepted* weight, both physically and mentally, he must now learn to *carry* it at walk, trot and canter.
2 We want to teach him the elementary language of the aids.
3 We shall introduce him to the first jumping lessons.
4 He must become more closely acquainted with the problems of traffic.

If the training progression was started early in April it should be possible to reach these final objectives by the end of August or mid-way into September.

The work and exercise periods during this time will be divided between lungeing, loose schooling, ridden work in the manege and hacking. For safety's sake, lungeing will always precede any ridden work.

All these activities are essential components of the last training stage and will be employed to produce variety in the horse's daily work.

If, for instance, we are still, as we should be, working two training sessions a day they will incorporate all, or most, of these activities. The morning session, which may now extend to as much as seventy-five minutes, interspersed with frequent rest periods, will include, perhaps, twenty-five minutes devoted to the lunge exercises and/or loose schooling, and the same amount of time can be spent on ridden work. The remaining twenty-five minutes will be used up in rest periods and the changing of the tack etc. The afternoon session can be devoted to straightforward hacking and a little traffic training. Later on, as we shall see, the ridden school work is largely replaced by a combination of work and exercise outside. That at least is the orderly way of arranging things, but, as usual, we must be flexible and not stick to a rigid timetable. Some days, to avoid monotony, we shall hack in the morning and school

19 and *20* A young pony has his
  first jumping lessons

after lunch. Frequently, we shall find it is the horse who decides for us what shall be done in the day. If, for instance, the
schooling period is not going well, which will happen from
time to time, no good purpose will be served by continuing.
We shall only make the horse resentful and more unco-
operative. In this situation it is better to go back to an easy
movement which the horse has already learnt, do it well once,
reward the horse with a pat and then spend the rest of the time
on a quiet hack, returning to the schooling on another day.

We may, indeed, find that our horse, quite definitely, 'goes
off' schooling and becomes distinctly unenthusiastic. If he
does so the fault will be ours – we shall have done too much
and sickened him of the whole business. The solution is to
forget about the manege for a week or so and spend our time
hacking in whatever open country is available to us. This is
not a time for the 'you b----- well will' attitude at all and we
are not being weak-minded by not insisting on the continuation of school work. What we are doing is recognizing that
we have made a mistake and are taking commonsense steps
to put matters right. In every stage of the training there is a

danger of hurrying on too fast, particularly if things seem to be going well, but nowhere is it more evident than in this early ridden work and it is something against which we should be constantly on guard.

Recognizing that the duration of exercise and work must be increased by gradual stages and that the activities mentioned are interlocking let us examine the work involved in each one of them and start with the ridden manege work.

In the School

At the end of Stage 6 the horse, wearing his saddle, bridle, side-reins, cavesson and riding reins, was being lunged on the elements of large circles with the rider in position and remaining almost entirely passive. He was being given an opportunity to accustom himself to the weight without being bothered by any aids. The only thing that is asked of the rider during these preliminaries is that she should change the diagonal at the trot according to which rein the horse is on.

This is a small point but an important one. To ride on the correct diagonal at trot on the circle entails the rider sitting in the saddle as the inside diagonal comes to the ground and rising as the opposite pair of legs touch down. The trot is a pace of two beats caused by the horse using first one diagonal pair and then, as it were, hopping on to the other one. The 'inside' diagonal on the circle left means the left (near) foreleg and the right (off) hindleg, the opposite being true for the circle to the right. There is a divergence of opinion as to whether it is better to sit on the inside or outside diagonal when riding a circle and in more advanced training an educated horseman may vary his use of the diagonal to achieve a specific object. However, as far as we are concerned, and it is the practice generally accepted in Britain (at least, that is, when anybody gives the matter thought), we shall sit on the inside diagonal. The reason for so doing, from the rider's viewpoint, is that it is easier to apply the inside leg, which will cause a greater engagement of the horse's corresponding hindleg, when sitting in the saddle than when one's bottom is in the act of being raised.

Clearly this is entirely relevant as far as the rider goes, but of far greater importance is the effect upon the movement of the horse. Unless the rider changes the diagonal frequently, even when riding on what seems to be a straight line, the horse becomes used to carrying the weight on one side of his back and so develops the muscles on that side, in order to cope with it, at the expense of the opposite set of muscles. The result is a one-sided horse, which is exactly what we have been trying to avoid from the beginning of our training, when all our exercises were directed at obtaining *equal* muscular development.

Off the Lunge

It is only a short step from the mounted horse circling the manege on the lunge to dispensing with the latter and going round on his own, although still controlled by the trainer's presence, his voice and, if necessary, the tactful use of his whip. As a preliminary to this, however, the rider must become more active and begin to apply simple and clearly defined aids. It is here that the trainer must ensure that his assistant applies those aids in the same manner as he himself will employ them in the future. There is no sense in teaching the horse to obey one set of instructions and then confusing him by using a slightly different set later on. The first aid we teach is that used to persuade the horse to **Go Forward**, and how often is this prime requirement neglected.

Right from the beginning we want to teach the horse to obey the lightest of indications given by the legs. If we start by giving the horse a resounding thump in the ribs with our heels to obtain a walk what strength of aids is going to be needed when we come to trot and canter? To start with, therefore, the horse is halted squarely on the lunge, the trainer standing fairly close to him, about ten feet or so away, in a line just to the rear of the hip.

At a word from him the rider **Prepares** the horse for the movement which is to be requested. To do so she applies her legs, quietly, in a pinching, rolling movement from rear to front, in effect a little nudge from the legs, at the same time as she makes a momentary closure of her fingers on the rein, which is still connected to the cavesson rings. The idea is to obtain the horse's attention, so that he is not caught flat-footed and unawares when the actual command is given. In effect this preparation is rather like that given by a Sergeant-Major to a squad of soldiers standing at ease. In his case, before he can give the command 'Quick March!', he must first give the order 'Atten-shun!' as an essential preparation for the movement. Almost immediately following the preliminary preparation the rider *yields* with her fingers, *acting* with both legs, just behind the girth, a fraction of a second later. The action of the legs at this time, and on every occasion in the future, must not be allowed to descend to a squeeze of clamp-like intensity, which means nothing to the horse at this or any other stage, nor, still less, must the legs *kick*. As before, the legs apply a definite rolling pinch from *rear* to *front*, but this time a shade more strongly than before – a push instead of a nudge. As the trainer sees the legs put on he gives the command 'Walk-on', and prepares to bring his whip into play as a further encouragement to obedience. Once the walk starts the rider's contact on the rein is gently taken up again and the legs continue to act with every stride. The most effective use of the legs at the walk is for them to be put on (from *rear* to *front*) alternately to coincide with the movement of the corresponding hindleg, causing it to be engaged more actively under the body.

When the horse moves off he must be allowed to go in a straight line; if we ask him to circle following the first step forward, we restrict the stride and, therefore, the free forward movement.

The aids so far described require, perhaps, some explanation, since they may appear strange to riders who previously have not given much thought to aid application when riding mature horses, not necessarily *trained* ones, who have become accustomed to certain general, if not always very logical, indications made by the hands and the legs.

From the beginning, let it be understood that the hands and legs operate in three distinct ways. They can **Act** to produce a particular result, they can **Yield** to reward obedience; one may yield to allow a request made by another or one may yield when another is required to predominate. Aids **Resist** when they are used to check an unwanted movement. In the aids so far the hand aid **Yielded** to allow the horse to move forward from the **Acting** legs. In simple terms the handbrake was released *before* the accelerator was depressed. The action of the legs, from *rear* to *front*, may also puzzle those who have so far been content to put the legs on and push *backwards*.

In the first place it seems more logical to push from rear to front, in the direction we want to go, if we want the horse to move *forward* but, more importantly, by using the legs in this way it prevents the horse from becoming confused when we apply them, in a different way, for other purposes.

If the legs are used from front to rear to get forward movement and then one of them is used in exactly the same way when we want the horse to move sideways, or to shift his quarters, how much more difficult it will be for the horse to differentiate between the two. Similarly, if we wish to hold the quarters, as when making a turn on them, we hold our legs, admittedly slightly more to the rear of the girth, in light contact with the flanks ready to resist any unwanted shift to either side. If then we have trained our horse to move forward by pushing our legs from front to back, and have trained him well, the slight movement of the legs to the rear could be interpreted by the horse as a request to move forward.

Every aid given must be quite distinct from any other if the horse is not to be confused. For this reason the use of the legs in the manner described is to be much commended.

The legs continue to act once the desired movement is obtained in order to maintain the impulsion and the evenness of the gait. In addition, by following this practice, we accustom the horse to moving from the leg up into contact with the hand. We ride him, in fact, by controlling the engine revs by means of the accelerator – riding from the back to the front, and not vice-versa.

The next aids to be taught on the lunge are those for halt. Do not, however, bother too much about it until the horse is obeying the aids to move off. Keeping the horse on a straight line, the trainer tells his assistant to halt. First, as before and as always, she prepares her horse by giving him an extra squeeze with both legs followed by a slight and momentary closing of both hands, the whole taking up no more than a second or so. Now she follows the same sequence as before of *yielding*, this time with the legs which, by ceasing to act, will cause the horse to slow down, and *acting* with the hands to bring the horse to halt. This will be more easily accomplished if her body is held upright, shoulders very slightly to the rear of the hips, which adds to the slowing effect by placing more weight on the quarters, whilst her hands act alternately on the reins, each squeeze being made as the foreleg corresponding to the hand is coming to the ground. Once the hands begin to act the legs are held passive, just in light contact with the horse's sides.

Perhaps, these aids need explaining, also; or at least the method of using the hand. By acting alternately on the rein we deny the horse a base against which he may learn to resist. A simultaneous action of both hands, particularly when employed in a sustained pull, has the opposite result to that which is wanted. By pulling we provoke a similar response in the horse, who motors on fighting to get away from the constant pressure of the hand. By applying the rein alternately we shall, when the rein is attached to the bit, produce a gliding motion across the mouth which allows the horse neither the time nor opportunity to resist. Further, if our hand acts as the leading leg is coming to the ground the movement of the head, which will be bent slightly towards it, will have the effect of closing the shoulder on that side and consequently shortening the stride which is being taken. Try it on a mature horse if you like – you will find that he comes to halt very much more easily.

The last thing to teach the horse on the lunge, before we let him go on his own, is the action of hand and leg on changes of direction to either hand. This we can do by working him on the usual circle, at the walk, with the rider employing the following aids.

Her inside leg will act just behind the girth in intermittent squeezes to encourage the greater engagement of the horse's inside leg and to assist in the lateral bending of his body. Her outside leg, held further behind the girth, remains in quiet

a

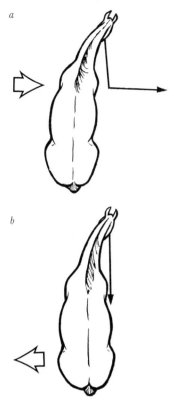

b

Figure 19
Two of the FIVE REIN EFFECTS.
(*a*) The simple DIRECT rein, the first rein effect, acting to turn the horse by moving the shoulders.
(*b*) The DIRECT rein of OPPOSITION, the third effect. The action of the rein blocks the forward thrust of the quarters, causing movement to be re-channelled, the quarters being pushed over to the left in order to make a turn to the right.

contact in support of the active leg and *resists* any inclination of the quarters to swing outwards and off the track made by the forelegs. The hands are used in the first of the five actions, the **Direct** or **Opening Rein**. The inside hand is carried out to the side, pulling the horse's nose in the required direction until it is possible to see the eye on that side. The outside hand *supports* its partner by being moved slightly forward to allow the bending of the neck and head. It must, however, remain in contact and, initially, it can help the shift of the shoulders by pushing intermittently against the withers. This is an exaggerated aid but to the horse its meaning is quite unmistakable. Later on we will employ the third rein action, the **Direct Rein of Opposition**, which entails the intermittent closure of the acting hand without it being carried out to the side, but the horse is not yet anywhere near ready for this rein effect, and at this stage it would only cause confusion, a restriction of the stride and loss of the essential forward progression. Throughout nearly the whole of the three-year-old phase we employ only this **Direct** rein effect.

Having taught these aids on the lunge at walk we teach the horse, still on the lunge, to make the transitions from walk to trot and back again and to execute a circle at trot whilst the rider, employing the same aids, sits on the inside diagonal.

The only new aid the horse has to learn is that given when we ask him to trot from walk. Again it must be quite different from that given to obtain the walk, since in future we will require him to go into trot from halt. The sequence is first, **Preparation**, made by a push with both legs accompanied by a brief closing of the fingers on a shortened rein. Secondly, the hands **Yield** and are immediately followed by both legs acting, quite strongly, from a position a good hand's breadth behind the girth and therefore to the rear of their position when giving the aid to walk. Once the horse breaks into trot the hands remain quite still in light contact whilst the legs continue to act together to maintain the impulsion and regularity of the pace. The hands must remain still at trot since the horse's head is held similarly; it does not move with each stride as in walk when our hands must, perforce, follow the movement continually if we are not to restrict the free, forward progress.

As in the lesson from halt to walk, the trainer will supplement the trot aid by his vocal command and since we will wish to use the whole manege, in order to take advantage of the straight line afforded by the long sides, he must be prepared to do some trotting himself. Should the horse increase the speed of the trot beyond what is required he must be checked by a predominant hand action, used alternately as before, whilst the legs cease to act. This continual action of the legs within a specific pace demands, indeed, a rider of some competence and tact. The usual mistake is to apply the aid too strongly. Once the pace is established at the required speed and rhythm (slow, please) only the very gentlest leg action is required. It is no more than an intermittent brushing of the coat by the lower leg. Now the horse is ready to be ridden off the lunge but still with the reins attached to the cavesson rings and still under the control of the trainer, who will keep himself in a handy position a few feet away from his pupil.

The first few lessons will consist of walking and trotting, using the whole manege area with the trainer moving himself into each corner in advance of the horse so that the latter walks or trots on his outside and cannot get into the habit of cutting the corners. At both walk and trot the rider must prepare her horse well in advance of their reaching the corner. She must begin her turning aids some two-thirds of the way down the long side so that the horse goes into the corner in the correct bend. Initially, the horse will have difficulty in bending through his corners at trot and we should not ask it of him before he can walk a corner correctly. In any case, the trot will need to be slowed down well before the corner, otherwise the horse will be forced to turn his head in the opposite direction, away from the movement, in order to maintain his yet insecure balance. Should he, in fact, start to bend his head and neck in this way persistently it is a sure indication that he is not yet ready for the movement and we should cease attempting it accordingly, concentrating on the walk and on allowing his balance and strength to improve before we return to it again. Changes of rein, in these first lessons, should be made at walk diagonally across the arena from and to the quarter markers. By this time the horse should be able to obey the rider without the support of the trainer's voice, the use of which will have been gradually reduced in the preceding lessons.

Even in these early days of the ridden work it is not too soon to take the young horse hacking on quiet lanes and bridle-paths in company with an older horse. This latter can walk alongside the youngster in the school for a few times, and the young horse can learn to be led from him in the school area.

The same system can be followed out hacking the trainer leading the young horse, who may be mounted, on the inside of his own steady horse. Obviously one would not expect to ride on roads where the traffic is constant so early on, but no harm will be done on quiet lanes, bridlepaths or over open country. The hacking exercise is not only of physical benefit to the horse but provides him with an interest and prevents him from becoming bored and stale. As a safety precaution fit a pair of knee-caps during these early outings.

Riding Off the Bit

In the school work the time has now arrived when the trainer can himself ride the horse, and complete his first phase of ridden training from the saddle.

To start with, the assistant can take over the trainer's role on the ground providing such encouragement and help as is necessary, but, within a few days, her presence will not be needed in the school, although she will still be called upon on occasions. The object now is to get the horse riding off the bit, which, if a mouthing bit with keys has been used, should be changed as soon as possible for something like a rubber snaffle.

For myself, if I had so far been using a rubber or vulcanite half-moon snaffle I would change it to a jointed snaffle, with a good, fat mouthpiece, within a week or so after I had got the horse riding on the bit. Although it is well worth making a gradual change from riding off the cavesson to riding from the mouth, there is no need for the process to be protracted.

With the side-reins removed the trainer can ride his horse with two reins, one fitted to the cavesson and the other to the bit. Within two or three days he can transfer control from one to the other, but for at least another week or so it is wise to retain the cavesson and its rein in case of emergency. If the horse should play up it is better to use the cavesson rein than the one connected to the mouth.

In the school exactly the same work will be carried out under the trainer as was done when the assistant rode the horse. The only difference will be that the trainer will be riding on the bit and concentrating on getting an ever quicker and more effective response from the horse. In particular, he will introduce the horse to the whip, that is, the long training whip which he will carry. The horse must not be made to fear the whip but he must come to accept its presence and respect it as an instrument which is brought into play to supplement his rider's legs. The great thing to achieve is to get the horse moving forward willingly and freely from a light leg pressure and in this a judicious use of the whip will be of great help.

First let the horse get used to the whip, tapping occasionally on his side just behind the leg. Because of its length this can be done without the rider taking his hand from the rein. It can then be used to sharpen the horse's reaction to the action of the legs telling him to move forward. For this exercise it is best to hold the reins in one hand advancing it well in front of the withers as the legs are applied to make the horse go from halt into walk. Immediately following the legs and almost before the horse has had time to obey, give him a sharp tap from the whip. The horse may move forward a little quicker than we anticipate but forward he will certainly go, and if our hand is already well to the front there should be no fear of touching his mouth. The horse should then be patted and made much of before this little exercise is carried out once more during the lesson. Thereafter he will remember and move forward from a very light shift of the legs, and an object has been achieved without any thumping or kicking.

21 Riding over a grid of poles

The remaining exercise to be done in the school is for the horse to be ridden at walk and trot over the poles and grid he crossed when on the lunge. This exercise will assist him in finding his balance under the rider's weight and is again a useful preliminary to mounted jumping. Its primary object remains, however, as before – the encouragement of the neck stretching and the engagement of the quarters. The rider must, therefore, allow his hands to yield to allow the extension and incline his body a little forward so as not to overload the quarters.

Once the horse performs the simple movements described within the school we can reduce the ridden work periods there and continue the schooling outside in the open country. Indeed, the sooner we are out of the school, within reason, the better. It is used only as a place to teach basic exercises and as a preparation for the work outside – *it is not an end in itself.* This is a matter to which too much emphasis cannot be given. Without hurrying, get out of the school and on to natural terrain as early as possible. The horse learns more and obtains greater physical and mental benefits from an hour's hacking than from twice that time spent in the manege. But, of course, he must have learnt the simple basic lessons of obedience first.

Hacking

This activity is, as you will now understand, really the most essential in this Stage. All the other exercises, the lunge and school work, are subservient to it, since the ability to ride the horse outside is the ultimate goal. The work in the school only prepares the horse for it and then only to a certain point.

To commence, ride out in company and always up to the end of this phase use an older horse as a companion and shield when riding in traffic. There will be no need for the young horse to be led any more but he can still not be regarded as being safe on the roads without the protection afforded by a steady, experienced escort.

Ride the young horse on a straight line at walk and trot, changing the diagonal frequently at the last pace, and do not bother about his head. Keep a contact throughout but let him carry it where and how he will. He needs it to make adjustments to his balance according to the nature of the ground he is passing over, and we must not interfere with this process. This is not to say that he may be allowed to slop along. Indeed, if we ride him as we did in the school with active legs and neck framed between the reins, pushing him forward into acceptance with his bit, he will be quite unable to move sloppily, and, furthermore, he will be under control. Choose ground which is uneven, and if you can find some fairly steep, short ascents and descents ride him quietly over these and make use, as well, of uphill slopes, up which you can trot. All this sort of country is ideal for developing muscle, strength and balance, but don't, for the moment, trot downhill, it will put too much strain on your horse. It will be soon enough to start trotting down gentle inclines towards the end of the phase when your horse is stronger and has better balance.

Every so often, if you can find a suitable corner of a field on which you are permitted to ride, practise making a few changes of direction, executing an odd circle or two and riding the occasional serpentine. Concentrate in these little schooling sessions, as at all other times, in maintaining an even rhythm in the pace, whether it is trot or walk. Do not neglect, however, to intersperse the session with frequent intervals of relaxation. After trotting, for instance, let the horse walk on a long rein with head and neck extended, but *keep* the contact and go on riding every second of every minute. Young horses have an endearing but not altogether comfortable habit of exploding when we least expect them to. However, do not let this deter you from letting him relax in this way. You are, in fact, expressing your trust in him, which is important and necessary. If he occasionally betrays that trust, or through no fault of his own is startled by a partridge getting up under his nose, there is always a good tuft of mane at hand to act as a life line.

Towards the end of the phase we can begin to alter our rein aid, changing from the direct, opening rein to the third effect (we will discuss the second effect in Chapter 15), This *direct rein of opposition* involves the use of the inside hand acting intermittently without being moved out to the side, although to start with a slight shift of both hands in the required direction will be helpful. The other hand is held as usual in support to prevent too great a bend occurring. The rein is termed 'of opposition' because it acts to block or oppose the forward movement of the quarters. 'Block', although a correct description in this context, does not mean that the rein 'stops' the forward movement. What happens is that it alters the direction of the thrust from the quarters. The thrust, being blocked by an opposing force, is compelled to shift its course; so, when we use the left rein, the thrust, unable to be delivered and to follow through because of the opposition of the rein, must, if it is maintained by the action of the legs, swing the quarters to the right, which is how the horse makes a left turn. This swing is converted into a bend by being controlled in extent by the action of the restraining, supporting outside leg. Remember that it is not the head and neck which dictate the direction taken by the horse – direction has its origin in the quarters. If the quarters, whether of their own volition or no, shift to the right, the horse turns to the left, and vice-versa. On the other hand, the head and neck, which, unlike the shoulders, are not directly connected with the quarters, may be turned to the right or left, whilst the horse turns in the opposite direction. But that is something which we will examine more carefully later on.

Another exercise to be introduced towards the end of the stage is that of speed-ups and slow-downs at walk and particularly at trot. At this stage it will be sufficient if we can obtain a longer stride by yielding with our hands whilst continuing to drive with our legs and a slightly shorter one by acting in the opposite fashion.

We must, also, before we finish with the horse and give him a rest through the Winter months, teach him the rudiments of the canter. We shall be doing some preparatory work for this pace on the lunge, but even before this there is no harm in letting our horse lollop along at a canter if he seems ready for it. Since the canter is a pace which excites the horse it is probably wiser to choose a slight uphill slope for our first attempts. There is no need to bother about the aids according to the book at this point, the horse won't have read them, anyway. Just go on driving with the legs, increasing the pace until the horse has to fall into canter in order to preserve his balance. The purpose of these first canters is to teach the horse how to carry weight at this new gait. We cannot expect a very polished performance, and we will find that most young horses will want to use our hands and the bit as a sort of fifth leg. This need cause no concern; all we have to do is to sit quietly, allowing him the freedom of his head and neck and interfering as little as possible. We must, however, continue to apply our leg aids according to which of the forelegs is leading. What we must not do is to get into the habit of cantering always at the same place, otherwise the horse will become excited every time he gets near to the cantering ground and will want to canter from force of habit and not because he has been asked to do so.

If we can find small ditches, a low log or a stream on our hacking expeditions we should take advantage of them, letting the older horse, if we have one with us, give the youngster a lead over these obstacles.

During hacking exercise we must expect our young horse to give vent to his high spirits by producing an occasional buck. This is a sign that the horse is feeling well and should be welcomed as such, but we must not let it get out of hand. Most horses seem to regard bucking as fun, and whilst we do not want to be spoil-sports we should recognize that if we allow it to take place too often it may become habitual. A buck on a cold morning may be taken in the spirit in which it is given but, beyond that, bucking must be corrected by raising the head *before* the buck has time to develop, and by driving the horse vigorously to the front with the legs, reprimanding him with our voice at the same time. If we always ride the horse with our legs, pushing him on to his bit, the chances of his being able to buck are naturally reduced, but this can sometimes be easier said than done. For the same reasons, a horse trained, as ours should be, to move forward from the leg should not find it possible to nap or jib – two small vices which are frequently present in the young horse when he is first ridden out on his own. It is in these respects that the value of a sound, basic school training is so apparent. A last word about bucking. Many young horses today are backed and schooled by young ladies, and a very good job some of them make of it, but in the main they are lightweights and they wear their coats fairly short, that is if they wear a conventional coat at all for informal riding. If you are one of these I would advise you, if you are thinking of showing the horse in ridden classes, or if you are making him for someone else, to get him used to being ridden by a man, who will (a) be heavier and (b) wear his coat tails longer.

When judging young hunters, on a number of occasions I have had some adventurous rides because the horse either resented my unaccustomed weight or couldn't abide my coat tails touching his back. Possibly it was a combination of both, but, for whatever reason, the result was unpleasant and naturally caused the horse to be put down the line. Do, I urge you, get your horse both man- and judge-proof.

Lungeing and Loose Schooling

Right through this stage, and indeed well into the four-year-old phase, the lunge work is continued and extended, and it should be a rule that the horse is always worked for ten minutes on the lunge before being ridden. There is no point in getting up on a fresh horse and risking a battle which you may lose by being deposited flat on your back, or which you may think you win by making use of the reins to maintain your position. In either case inestimable damage will have been done and it could have all have been so easily avoided by spending a few moments putting the horse into a more receptive frame of mind by using the exercise of the lunge.

22 Riding over a grid of low cavalletti

The forms of lungeing which we now carry out are extensions of those practised in the preceding stages and are directed at strengthening our horse and improving his balance and outline. The canter work is begun and we start teaching the horse to jump. We have already established the work over a grid of poles and can now induce even greater activity in the horse by replacing the poles with cavalletti. Place these first, having removed the side-reins, at their lowest height, spaced at the trotting distance as previously, and gradually work up to crossing them at their maximum height. The horse should move over the grid with active, elevated steps at trot, and with a noticeable engagement of the hocks. The back will be well rounded and the head and neck – the latter now showing considerable muscular development on its top-line – will be stretched out and forwards.

The work on the flat in the side-reins is continued, and again it is the rounded form that we are seeking, with the horse reaching forward to make contact with the bit. Whether the side-reins can now be shortened a hole or two and fixed on the middle dees of the roller depends very much on the development of our pupil. A big, well-grown chap with a good hard top on his neck will allow us to shorten up a few holes and begin to show the first signs of a nicely raised head carriage. Be careful, however, and after a few minutes work on the shortened reins let them out again so that he can relax by stretching out the head and neck once more. The period of work on the shorter reins can be increased, gradually, day by day, but watch particularly for any faint hint of overbending. Watch also the ears – if he carries one down and one up he is twisting his head at the poll. That means that he is uncomfortable and that your side-reins are too tight. Again, the head should be carried steady; any waving about is a sign of resentment. With a late developer, noticeably lower at the wither than at the croup, it is better to continue with the long side-reins and leave any shortening experiments until the following year. To shorten now will only lead to a faulty head-carriage and a possibly hollowed back.

Head-carriage is the result of increased engagement of the hocks, placing the weight further towards the quarters and lightening the forehand – side-reins, as mentioned before, are at best no more than assistants to this process.

Following the grid work, which is still carried out on a straight line, we may ask the horse to make his first jump. If we have a grid of four cavalletti this jump can be made by removing cavelletto three and placing it on top of cavalletto four, leaving a distance of between 10 and 12 feet between the first two and the final small fence. By turning the last cavalletto to its middle height we shall have made a jump about 20 inches high which is sloped away from the take-off and has a spread of about the same measurement. We want the horse to jump this from trot, which entails his using the whole of his body, rather than from canter, but should he make a few strides at canter on landing this is all to the good and may be permitted, although we shall always bring him back to walk and halt before circling near the fence and asking him to jump it again.

The Canter on the Lunge

We can also use a cavalletto to teach the canter on the lunge. Place it just before a corner of the school and let the horse approach (without side-reins) at a good, strong trot. Almost inevitably the horse will strike-off into canter on landing and will lead with the inside foreleg. Be content to obtain a few good canter strides, allowing the horse freedom of his neck and head, then bring him back to trot before tackling the exercise again. This must be practised on both reins until the canter is performed calmly and with the correct lead.

If we give the vocal command 'Cann-terr!' each time the horse lands we shall in time be able to obtain the canter at the corner of the school without the help of the cavalletto. To do so, smoothly, or relatively so, however, we must employ a little technique. The knack is in sending the horse into the corner already bent in the direction of the movement. As he comes at trot down the long side we use our voice, hand and whip to steady him and bring him together. Giving the soothing command 'steady', which by now he should well understand, we resist with our hand, by giving little intermittent squeezes on the rein, and continue with the utmost tact to push him on by making slight movements with our whip. Having obtained an active, slow trot, we may then bend the head slightly towards us, raising the hand to free the horse's inside shoulder, as we give the command to canter.

The circles at canter must necessarily be large which will involve movement on the part of the trainer – no pivot-on-the-heel nonsense – and, if necessary, we must sacrifice the circle in order to keep the horse moving forward without restriction. If the horse has difficulty in completing an element of the circle do not pull him round. Instead, release your rein and let him go straight for a few strides. If he hangs on the rein the circle is too tight for him and you must make it larger. Should the horse set off too fast for comfort check him with your voice supported by the rein which must incline his head towards the leading foreleg as each stride begins. The effect of this action is to inhibit the full movement of the inside shoulder and therefore to reduce the length of the stride.

At this stage if the horse can strike off into canter on either leg and maintain the pace in calm for one large circuit, not necessarily a perfect circle, this will be enough. We can ask for a more polished performance in the side-reins in his secondary education as a four-year-old.

Loose Schooling

Providing the horse is obedient to the voice, loose-schooling presents no difficulties. As the ultimate exercise in obedience and discipline it is very valuable, and by employing it we can teach the horse to think for himself when jumping and increase his confidence in his own ability.

To school loose we shall find that the full area of the manege is too large and that the horse will be more easily controlled if we cut off one end of the area. It won't be possible to rail off the unwanted piece with an unjumpable barrier, but this is not necessary. The psychological effect of a line of cavalletti with a rope stretched over the top and marked with bits of rag tied on at intervals is normally quite sufficient.

To a great degree the success of loose-schooling depends upon the trainer positioning his body intelligently and anticipating the movements of his pupil.

Obviously, we should not attempt to school loose until our horse has been made calm and obedient by a little work on the lunge. Initially one will find that the horse tends to fall continually towards the centre and to cut the corners. This can be prevented by the trainer moving on a circle within that made by the horse and pushing the latter out to the track by means of his whip. Don't be afraid to work close to your horse. All horses seem to enjoy this loose work and many are amazingly co-operative. Indeed, I have never met a horse, who having been made obedient on the lunge, cannot be persuaded to work equally well without its restraint. When the horse is obedient we can carry out all over again the exercises over the cavalletti grid and we can begin jumping.

For this purpose make two fences, one small upright and one spread fence, and place them on opposite sides of the ring. These two fences each call for a different approach. The upright has to be approached on a comparatively short stride and it encourages a horse to stand back if he is not to get under the fence and attempt an impossibly steep angle of ascent. The spread fence, a very valuable one, can be jumped off a longer stride and causes the horse to extend himself on a slightly flatter trajectory. It increases the scope of the horse when jumping.

The upright can be gradually raised to around 2 feet 3 inches and to help the horse a ground pole can be placed at the same distance on the ground in front of the fence to give him a point

Figure 20a
Arrangement of cavalletti making the final element a jump.

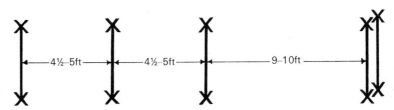

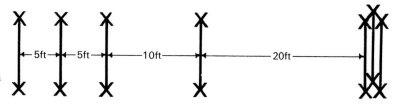

Figure 20b
A variation, showing the introduction
of two correctly spaced jumps.

of take-off and assist him in judging his stride. An additional
aid is a placing fence, such as a cavalletto, sited some 33 feet
(two jumping strides at canter) in advance of the upright.
This will have the effect of steadying the horse and will prevent
him rushing his fences as well as helping him to judge the distance involved. The upright should, of course, be solid. We do
not want to hurt our pupil in any way but equally he must
learn, for his own good, to respect a fence. One built of thin
poles, easily dislodged, and with a lot of daylight visible
through it will produce a careless jumper and is, indeed, not
nearly so easy to jump! Fixed railway sleepers with a stout
pole on the top, which will take a good knock before falling,
is the best type of upright schooling fence.

The spread should be equally solid in its first element and
beyond this we can place a good pole some 6 inches higher
than the first part, extending the spread by degrees up to
2 feet 6 inches. The height of the fence (at the final pole) need
not exceed 2 feet 3 inches. This is an easy fence to jump and
is made even more so if the first element is sloped away from
the ground line. Again it will be an advantage to provide a
placing fence. These fences, which to begin with will be very
low, are best jumped from trot. At the trot pace the horse is
compelled to engage his hocks and will more easily obtain a
rounded form over the jump. If he is allowed to go fast, at
canter, the jump flattens and height is lost. He *learns* how to
jump out of trot and the exercise assists in the strengthening
and suppling process. To work the horse at trot over the fences
the trainer must work reasonably close and be in a position to
encourage the horse in the approach to the fence.

One has to bear in mind all the time the triangles of control
and imagine that the horse is still attached to the hand by the
lunge. If the arena is not too large control will be made easier.
It is only when one becomes too far separated from the horse
physically that control becomes difficult.

From the beginning the horse must be prevented from rushing. The placing fences will help considerably in this but after
each jump the horse must be persuaded to come back to walk
or even halt before being presented at the next one. It may,
indeed, be necessary for the trainer to move across the arena
in order to interpose his body between the horse and the next
fence, in order to get the horse jumping each fence on com-

mand alone rather than indulging in a wild circus-like steeple-chase. Both fences should be constructed so that without too much effort they can be changed to allow the horse to jump them from either rein.

It is, of course, absolutely essential that the horse's legs are protected adequately, as they should be whenever he is being worked.

Completion of Phase 1

Somewhere between the end of August and mid-September the primary education of the three-year-old will be completed and it will be time to give the horse a rest. He should be in fairly big condition by now with a good muscular development and, we hope, still one hundred per cent sound.

He should not, however, be thrown out in a field and for-gotten for the Winter. The process of roughing off must be gradual, the exercise and work period being decreased whilst the period spent at grass each day becomes a little longer. His shoes can be removed and, if it is thought necessary, replaced with tips to prevent the feet breaking.

By the end of September, most certainly, he should be out of work and spending the best hours of daylight in his pad-dock, being stabled at night. The horse will need feeding in the same quantity to which he has become accustomed in order to encourage maximum growth but otherwise leave him alone to grow and relax. The importance of good and gener-ous feeding during this break cannot be emphasized too much. He needs the best of food; good oats, linseed mashes, and an additional cod-liver oil supplement to encourage bone growth as well as being given as much good quality hay as he will eat. When we bring him into work again in the following April we want a big, strong horse in first-rate condition, and he will not be this unless he is well-fed and managed over the Winter.

Before putting the horse out make sure that the worming programme has been kept up to date and have his teeth checked by the vet. You have already spent a deal of time and money on the animal and there is no sense in spoiling the ship for a ha'porth of tar.

Chapter 12   The Long Reins

For the very good reason that the long reins do not play a part in this training progression, this chapter, in which their use is discussed, is sandwiched in a state of limbo between those dealing with the two phases of schooling.

There are, basically, four distinct schools of long-reining. (1) The Danish Manner, exemplified by the performance, at the Horse of the Year Show in 1966, of Miss Sylvia Stanier, who is a pupil of that great Master, E. Schmit-Jensen, in which the rein passes from the mouth through the terrets of a harness pad to the trainer's hand over the horse's back. (2) The Classical method, used at the Spanish School and elsewhere, in which the rein passes from the mouth directly to the trainer's hands, the trainer being positioned immediately behind and hard up against the animal's rear. (3) The French Manner, where the reins come from the mouth through ring terrets on a driving collar and then drop down through rings placed midway on a breaking roller and thence to the trainer's hand. The trainer stands behind the horse. (4) The British method, which varies delightfully according to individual preference or the variety of equipment available. In its more sophisticated form the reins pass from the bit through rings midway on the roller and are held by the trainer standing behind. In the more slap-dash style a saddle is worn and the reins are passed through the stirrup irons, which are run up the leathers.

The first system, the Danish Manner (employing the reins over the back), can be used to drive the horse straight forward or to work him on circles. In hands as expert as Miss Stanier's the horse can be made to produce the full range of High School movements without ever having the rider on his back. The hands, however, need to be expert and I do not imagine that one average horseman in a hundred could employ the method satisfactorily without having received practical instruction.

The Spanish School method is again out of the reach of all but the most dedicated professionals and, whilst it may be safe enough to stand so close to the back end of a docile Lippizaner, I would not recommend that it should be attempted with a young English Thoroughbred.

Some examples of Long
Reining
23 The English method
24 The Danish method

25 The classical Spanish method

The French method is used to assist the horse in obtaining *Ramener*, the high and near vertical head-carriage caused by the body advancing towards the head and is, therefore, not applicable in the elementary training with which we are concerned. It could, however, be employed usefully in the last stages of the four-year-old training phase providing that the trainer was sufficiently skilled.

Finally the British method, which is specifically intended for the elementary training of the horse, and is, therefore, the one with which we should be most concerned. The object is to 'mouth' the horse, increase his handiness and confirm him in the forward movement. The horse may be driven straight ahead or on a circle, when the outside rein will always encircle his body passing back to the hand from a point just above the hock. The same will, of course, apply when the horse makes a shallow turn with the trainer walking directly behind. In theory there is nothing to which exception might be taken providing that proper tackle is used. The method of passing the

Figure 21
The arrangement of the long reins
in the French manner.

rein through the irons is not very sensible and frequently results in a rein becoming jammed. In practice, however, I am
not sure that it achieves anything more than can be obtained
following the progression outlined, and there are several very
big 'ifs' and 'buts'. It is possible to get the horse responding
to the bit, *if* the hands are sufficiently sensitive, and they need
to be those of an angel; but the very weight of the reins is a
disadvantage and a more serious one occurs on the circle when
the horse tends to lean his whole weight on the encircling outside rein and consequently on that side of his mouth.

Is the horse's mouth any better for long-reining than it is
at the end of our first three-year-old phase? Personally, I
doubt it, and it may indeed be much worse – so much depends
on the hands *and* the agility and wind of the trainer. Is the
horse any handier? To that I think the answer is no. The long-
reined horse may respond to the bit but ours responds to *both*
bit and legs.

On the last point I would agree that it is a good way of confirming forward movement *without* the rider being on the
horse's back. On the other hand, the progression we have discussed confirms forward movement no less, and under saddle
as well. The argument that a horse benefits from being driven

in long reins on the roads and through traffic may still be tenable in some parts of the country, but in my quiet corner of Constable's East Anglia it would be tantamount to sudden death.

I do not for a moment deny that there are some highly-skilled trainers who obtain excellent results from long-reining, but they are *highly-skilled* and may even be able to drive a youngster down Regent Street in the rush hour in absolute safety. They, however, are the exception and there are plenty more who are not nearly so expert. Just take a look at the gentlemen involved in Plate 26.

26 How not to do it – the worst sort of English long-reining

I admit to being biased about the long reins, or at least the British method of using them. I believe I can get a better result from the saddle without them. I would certainly use long reins if I was schooling a horse for harness but not when training a riding horse. But there, I'm not very good at it and as I said – I'm biased. (At least I am in good company, Henry Wynmalen didn't use long reins either.) The only exception I would make would be in the case of ponies too small for an adult to ride. Then the long-reins can be of value in teaching changes of direction, furthering the forward movement obtained on the lunge and, if the hands are skilful enough, getting the pony on to and accepting his bit.

Part Two

Chapter 13   Secondary Education

The second Phase in the education of the young horse begins in the April of his fourth year. If all has gone well there should be a pronounced difference in the physical appearance between the three-year-old and the more developed four-year-old. By this time, the cumulative effect of good feeding over a period of years, together with the training that has been done, should have resulted in a big, well-grown, strong young horse.

However, it would be a mistake to put our horse straight into new work; as usual, he must be prepared gradually if we are to avoid the risk of sprains and strains. Accordingly, the first few weeks are spent quietly in a complete recapitulation of the ground covered in Phase 1, during which he should be wormed and have his teeth inspected. It is advisable to spend at least the first week on the lunge line before attempting to ride the horse, rather than presume too much on one's pupil's good nature. Frequently there will be little trouble experienced, but it has to be recognized that, if anything, this is the more difficult of the two phases.

The horse is rather like a small boy, who, for his first term, works away diligently and is far too much in awe of his teachers and surroundings for any thoughts of rebellion to enter his head. But, by the time the lad is in his second term this desirable respect for authority is wearing a little thin. Familiarity encourages him to try out his new-found assurance and he begins to assert himself. Horses, in this respect, are not much different, and we have to be prepared for exuberance and, on occasions, outright disobedience.

It is, therefore, of the greatest importance that we should consolidate the work of the first phase, insisting quietly on obedience from the horse in the exercises which he has already learnt, before attempting to teach anything new.

As before, we will define the objectives to be reached in the four-year-old phase. By the end of December, a period of some eight months, we are aiming to produce a well-conditioned, balanced horse, obedient and comfortable to ride. He will need to be safe in traffic and should have learnt to jump a variety of reasonable obstacles, including coloured fences. In fact, we want an all-round horse who, in his fifth year, will be able to take us hunting for a full season and will be able to compete creditably in small events.

This is our overall objective, which again is comprised of a number of subsidiary ones. The order in which these are given is not necessarily chronological since, as in the previous phase, overlapping must necessarily occur.

1   Progressive physical conditioning, which is the result of combining the three prime elements of **Grooming**, **Feeding** and **Exercise** in the correct measure.
2   The furtherance of the horse's mental development.
3   Placing the horse on the bit and in hand.
4   Increase of both lateral and longitudinal suppleness by gymnastic exercises.
5   Teaching the horse the aids up to the secondary standard.
6   Inducing a greater degree of straightness in the horse, which will involve the perfecting, as far as that is possible, of the simpler school exercises and figures.
7   Continuing and extending the jumping training, concentrating on getting our horse to jump correctly, calmly and in the proper rounded form.
8   Once we have obtained obedience to leg and hand teaching the horse reliability in traffic by a greater exposure to varied road conditions.
9   Making the first introduction to the double bridle.

Once more we will break down the progression into stages, each one being a logical preparation for the next.

Before studying the work involved in detail, however, we should be quite clear what we mean by *physical conditioning*, which in this phase is carried out to a higher degree. It is important because it is upon the *correct* conditioning of the horse that everything else depends.

Basically, condition is the result of **Feeding**, **Grooming** and **Exercise** supplied in the correct balance, and that is the answer one would expect to receive from any Pony Club member who was questioned on the subject. In reality it is more complex.

The majority of horse-owners, of average intelligence and experience, given time and having at hand sufficient quantities of good food will be able to produce a fit, muscled, healthy horse. But, and this is at the grass roots of conditioning, if the muscles are developed *incorrectly* and are not made supple there is little to applaud in the achievement. Should the physical build-up be made on a badly-laid foundation – a wrong overall shape – fitness and muscular development will serve only to confirm the incorrect form. We may have produced a fit horse but it will not be a mechanically efficient one.

Without full and proper muscular development, maximum flexion of the joints is impossible and the structure is subjected to a greater strain.

Once a horse has been made fit without due regard being paid to the correctness of his form it is an almost impossible task to break down the strong but badly designed shape and to re-build it on acceptable lines. We must, therefore, be sure that the development of the muscular complex and of the essential rounded form is given absolute priority. By doing so, we shall avoid a hundred and one resistances, which come about because the horse is so built that it causes him discomfort to perform the movements we require.

The health of the horse depends on the quality and quantity of his food; the standard of his general living conditions; the efficiency with which he is groomed and, of course, on the exercise he receives. All should be of the highest quality if our horse is to do well. Poor food does no good, lazy grooming is next to no grooming and exercise badly performed, confirming existing faults instead of trying to eradicate them, is retrograde in the extreme.

As a guide, we should aim by the end of September to be getting at least two and a half hours work and exercise done each day. Excluding the early morning quartering, the grooming period should not be less than forty-five minutes and the horse's rations can rise to as much as 10–12 lb of concentrates and about 16–18 lb of hay, if he stands about 16 h.h. As always, the exercise and work periods and the rations must be increased by gradual stages. There is no sense in putting up with a silly over-fed horse who, in any case, will be inattentive. The solution is to cut back the corn ration until he becomes more sensible, or alternatively to increase the exercise period by a reasonable amount. In practice a combination of both will be found to have the desired effect.

In the following chapters, the stages in Phase 2 are discussed in detail with the exception of Stage 1, which is simply a period of recapitulation and consolidation of the primary education carried out in the first phase but which must be carried out thoroughly before attempting anything else. In addition, of course, it acts as a physical and mental preparation for the more arduous work which follows.

Earlier I stressed the fact that the trainer can only teach within the compass of his own knowledge. In this phase the truth of this assertion becomes increasingly apparent, and it underlines the necessity of learning to ride (both in theory and practice) before attempting the education of the young horse. So often, young riders will complete Phase 1 quite satisfactorily, but then come to a full stop in the second year of training because they have reached the limit of their own knowledge and are at a loss to know what they should do next. In these cases, the education of the horse stops when the limitation of the rider is reached and further progress is impossible. As a result the rider, and the world at large, is left with a half-schooled horse. Temperament and physical ability in the individual horse will naturally limit the extent to which he can be schooled, but if the trainer has taken the trouble to equip himself as well as he is able, *before* tackling the task of teaching the young horse, there is no reason why the finished product should not be within reach of his maximum potential at the completion of the four-year-old phase.

Chapter 14

Phase 2, Stage 2: On the Bit

In this stage lungeing, ridden work and hacking (exercise) are again blended into the training progression, but for the sake of clarity it is best to examine these three elements as separate entities.

Lunge

In the lunge work, which still forms the basis of the ridden exercises, we continue and extend the exercises over the cavalletti grid and we also work at trot, endeavouring to obtain a correct bend for longer periods. The same method is employed as before in the use of the side-reins, but it should be possible to work the horse on the shortened reins, attached to the highest dees of the roller, for increasing lengths of time.

27 Lungeing off the bit

The lunge work will also include short jumping sessions – designed to encourage confidence, freedom and good style – and a little work at canter.

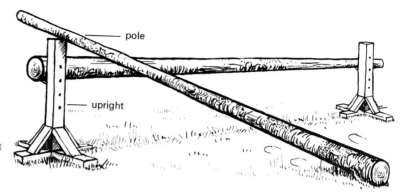

pole

upright

Figure 22
The use of a pole laid on the upright so as to prevent the line being caught on the latter when lungeing a horse over a small fence.

When jumping a horse on the lunge using the conventional uprights, it is advisable to rest a pole on the top of the upright, with the other end on the ground towards the take-off side of the fence. The pole itself should extend some 18 inches beyond the top of the upright. The purpose of this device is to prevent the lunge-rein from catching on the upright. Without this precaution the rein can easily become fouled, with consequences that are easily imagined. Make the fences stout, firm and solid, working up to no more than 2 feet 6 inches in height and incorporate a spread of the same measurement, put down a ground pole in front of the fence to assist the horse and use a 'distance' pole or low cavalletto 33 feet away to act as a further assistance in judging the distance and also to prevent the horse getting into the habit of rushing. The procedure is just as before. First, circle alongside the fence until the horse is calm and obedient then ask him to approach from a strong trot and to jump from that pace.

The object is to produce a horse whose shape over the fence follows a definite arc, which entails, of course, a lowered head and neck and a rounded back, and to develop scope in the leap. Jumping in this form, particularly from trot, encourages the horse to raise his forelegs naturally, and at no time will it be necessary to employ the insidious rapping pole or any other such device. If the horse tends to use himself insufficiently and to make too steep a descent, place a pole on the ground a foot or so on the landing side, or even put down a low cavalletto. This will cause him to stretch over his fence in order to avoid landing on the final element. Should he break into a stride or two of canter on landing, allow him to do so, but bring him back to walk as soon as it is possible. When the horse is jumping confidently vary the fences by introducing uprights, or by adding straw bales or painted drums. As most horses will look twice at coloured fences it is as well to begin using more and more brightly painted poles. He has to get used to them and the earlier in the training he starts jumping coloured fences the more commonplace they will become.

Previously, we practised the canter departs by lungeing the horse over a cavalletto placed at the entrance to a corner. We can continue, for a while, to use this aid, only now we must ask for rather more than the one or two strides that satisfied us at the end of the previous phase. Do not, however, for the moment expect to get a full and well-formed circle. Be content with a half-circle, allowing the horse to straighten for a few strides when he has completed it, before bringing him back to trot.

In a few lessons, making judicious use of the schooling area and the 'canter' cavalletto, you should be able to get a half-circle at canter at either end of your school with the whole figure looking something like an oval shape. Remember to lengthen your side-reins for canter work, and be sure that your hand gives immediately before the first canter stride, to allow unrestricted movement of the inside shoulder.

On the Bit and In Hand

Throughout the lungeing sessions time will be spent encouraging the horse to continue reaching forward for his bit in the side-reins. Now it is time to go a stage further and begin the work of putting him in hand, and there is a vast deal of difference between the two.

28 The first obedience under saddle, the horse remaining immobile whilst being mounted

139

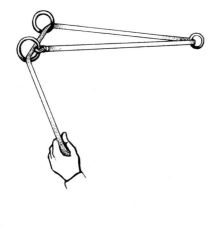

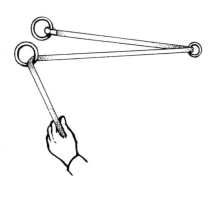

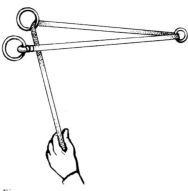

Figure 23
The three methods of fastening the lunge rein when lungeing from the bit with the object of placing the horse on the hand. The first is the most commonly used since equal tension is applied on the mouth, the other two are ways of correcting a faulty bend in the neck.

On the side-reins he learnt to make and accept contact with the bit, now he must learn to make and accept contact with the hand, which, unlike the side-reins, can yield and resist to an infinite and subtle degree.

By using the hand directly in contact with the mouth, the horse can be pushed up to it with far greater effect than by using side-reins, which lack the power of easement, to 'pull the horse together'.

In most cases it is inadvisable to do other than condemn the practice of lungeing from the bit. But, for the horse who has gone through the suggested progression it is a logical step forward and is far safer and more effective than 'making a mouth' from the long reins or, at this stage, from the saddle. Tools and methods, admittedly, are only as good or as bad as the trainer who uses them, but there is certainly less risk involved in employing the methods I am going to describe, than there are in hanging on to long reins. Indeed, there are specific advantages in these methods which will not be found in others.

To put the horse on the hand it is necessary to make use of the loose forward set ring on the front of the roller, which was mentioned in Chapter 5. In addition, a considerably longer lunge line of lighter weight is needed. Possibly the best way out of this difficulty is to get a saddler to make up a light, tapered, nylon plough line with a loop at one end and a light snap hook at the other. It should be about 6–8 feet longer than the usual line. The fact that the line is of rope, which can burn the hand painfully should it be pulled through the fingers, is not relevant at this stage since our horse should be well used to working quietly on the lunge.

There are three positions for the exercise of which numbers one and three (see Figure 23) are required the most frequently. To be effective, however, a great deal depends upon the small ring strap on the roller being of the correct length, and it is as well if this can be adjusted an inch or two either way. If the strap is too long, it will only allow the rein to frame a part of the neck instead of the whole, and this framing of the neck is immensely important if the latter is to become our piece of tempered steel rather than the piece of too-flexible rubber, that will frustrate all our efforts. On the other hand, too short a strap causing the rein to be anchored too close to the roller will result in a 'caving-in' of the neck in front of the withers and all the horrors that ensue.

In the first position the rein causes the bit to operate evenly on both sides of the mouth; the horse should be well accustomed to the rein thus positioned before any use is made of the other two, which are largely corrective in their purpose. In the diagram of position one, the rein is shown fitted for the circle left and the opposite manner of adjustment is used for a right-handed circle.

It should not be necessary if the horse has been well worked to either hand to employ the second position, but it is useful for correcting a spoilt horse.

The third position, used to prevent any inclination towards the centre, will in all probability be needed to perfect the making of a *real* circle, as most horses, on one rein or the other, will have a slight tendency to fall inwards. Clearly, the rein must be used with great tact, and the more skilful the trainer the better the result. There is, however, no need to be frightened of using this method providing you remember, first that the hand must act intermittently all the time and yield in accordance with the responses of the horse, and secondly that your whip must cause the horse's body to advance into contact with the hand, instead of the hand forcing a retraction of the head and neck. The acceptance of and response to the bit must come as the result of the thrust and engagement of the quarters.

If we have succeeded in stretching the neck sufficiently, its contraction and the higher attitude it now should begin to adopt will be made easily and naturally. It is most important that we should not ask for a higher head-carriage from the saddle, until the horse can obtain it on the lunge without the added burden of our weight.

Ridden Schooling

The school work at this stage consists of little more than polishing up the aid lessons, continuing the neck stretching exercises and commencing to teach the horse to jump under saddle.

Employing the simplest of the school figures, changes of rein made diagonally across the school, shallow curves and the occasional circle using half the school area, we should be able to make directional changes by using the Third Rein Effect, the *Direct Rein of Opposition*, which was discussed in the closing stages of the last phase (see p. 118). If the horse is resistant to its use, then return for a day or so to the simple opening rein and in the meantime check the application of your aids.

By using the Third Rein Effect, which acts on the quarters to alter the direction of the forward movement, the horse bends round the turn along the whole length of the body. Or, at least, he does so if the rider's aids are operating correctly. For instance, on the turn to the left, the action of the left hand employed in the Third Rein Effect bends the head to the left, thus blocking the thrust of the quarters and causing them to

141

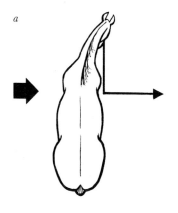

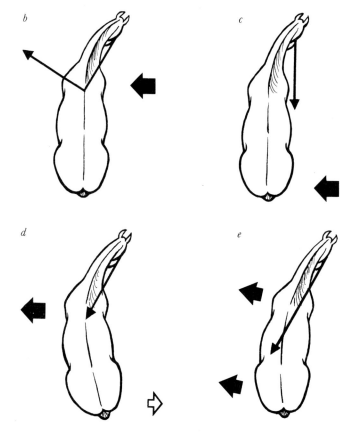

Figure 24
The FIVE REIN EFFECTS. (*a*) The simple DIRECT rein, (*b*) The simple INDIRECT REIN, (*c*) The DIRECT REIN OF OPPOSITION, (*d*) The INDIRECT REIN OF OPPOSITION in *front* of the withers, (*e*) The INDIRECT REIN OF OPPOSITION *behind* the withers (the intermediary rein). The black arrows indicate the primary movement, the open ones the secondary movement.

shift to the right and therefore altering the direction of the movement. The right hand supports the action of the left, by advancing slightly to allow for the bending of the head (without allowing that bend to become too pronounced). It is in fact *resisting* any such inclination.

The left leg, in the turn to the left, *acts* on the girth to maintain the impulsion and also to assist the directional change taken by the quarters in response to the rein effect. The right leg is used, and most importantly, to hold the quarters on the track made by the forelegs. It, therefore, can be said to *resist* the outward movement of the quarters; a movement which if not controlled by the action of the right leg would result in them being carried outside the track made by the forelegs. To achieve this objective the right leg must therefore be carried to the rear of the girth, being placed flat against the horse and *resisting*, if necessary, by inward pushes. In the schooled horse, the results of these aids will be to produce in the turn a uniform bend of the horse from poll to tail, giving the appearance of the horse being 'bent round the rider's inside leg'. I say 'the *appearance* of being bent . . .' because in fact the deepest point of the arc formed is not, and cannot be, in a line with the position of the rider's leg, for the reason that the horse's spine is a pretty rigid structure, a degree of flexibility only being possible in the area of the lumber vertebrae, behind the saddle. What, in fact, is happening is that the inside of the horse flattens, whilst the outside, taking up the curve enforced by the directional change, is pushed outwards by the stretching of the large muscles on that side. The horse then 'appears' to be bent round the inside leg.

To date we have been concerned with the aids *acting* and *yielding*. Now we add to them a further dimension, that of *resistance*.

Just as legs can *resist* so can our hands, but they must do so with infinite tact if they are not to interrupt the flow of forward movement obtained through our legs, and before we allow them to operate in this role we must have first obtained complete obedience to the action of both legs urging the horse to go forward.

The immediate forward movement of the horse in response to the action of the legs is so important that it cannot be stressed too much. Throughout the training we must ensure that this vital requirement is met. Should our horse at any moment be reluctant to respond to the leg then we must have recourse to the long training whip to reinforce the leg signal. Giving the horse a couple of sharp taps with the whip immediately following the application of the legs, or indeed almost simultaneously with this action, is far better than indulging in heel thumping and contributes to immediate response from the *lightest* of pressures given by the leg. Without having obtained response of this quality any resistance by the hand results only in a diminution of impulsion.

At this stage resistance by the hands is minimal, and the principal purpose is to reduce the time lapse between the act and yield sequence of the aids. However, we can begin to 'prepare' our horse for the various movements rather more definitely by preceding transitions, changes of direction, etc., by acting with our legs and allowing our hands to resist momentarily at the same time. The effect of these actions results ultimately in a shortening of the horse's outline and is a means of suppling his body longitudinally. We should be compressing the horse towards his centre by maintaining the thrust forward from the hindquarters at one end, and holding, or *resisting*, that impulsion at the other, a sort of both ends against the middle exercise.

Initially, no noticeable degree of shortening will take place and the slight resistance of our fingers, whilst our legs continue to act, will serve only as a warning to our pupil that he should give us his attention in preparation for an alteration in pace or direction. This slight resistance of the hand, even at this early stage, will, however, induce a little alteration in the balance of the horse – the weight being placed more to the rear than on the fore-hand. This process puts the horse into a better position to respond to the change being requested, since there will be a greater engagement of the driving force provided by the hindlegs and a subsequent, if only slight, lightening of the fore-hand.

Our sequence of aids then becomes **Preparation**, preceding each request, followed by **Yielding** and **Acting** on the part of legs or hands and also the third function of the aids, **Resistance**. For instance, if we wish to go from walk into trot we prepare the horse by pressing on with our legs, into hands that resist intermittently and then follow this action by yielding with the hands and continuing the action of the legs to push the horse into the faster pace.

It has to be recognized though, that in teaching the horse to respond to the lightest of aids there is a danger that he will anticipate by responding, perhaps not in the way we require, to *any* movement of the leg and hand. If we are to avoid this sort of situation, we have to be capable of giving aids which, though light, are quite clearly defined, otherwise our horse will become confused. This is why earlier in the training sequence we insisted that the aids for trot (both legs be applied from rear to front) should be given with rather more intensity and somewhat behind the position employed when we wanted the horse to move into walk from halt. The object was that, when we eventually asked for trot from halt, the horse should be quite clear in his mind as to what was wanted.

In the case of making the transition from walk to trot, which is what we are presently concerned with, we have to take care lest the action of our legs in the phase of preparation should cause the horse to break into trot before the predetermined point of departure from the one gait to the other has been reached. To avoid this, it seems more satisfactory to prepare the horse by increasing the impulsion of the walk by separate, instead of combined, actions of each leg or hand as we discussed in the last stage of the three-year-old phase. If we have developed sufficient 'feel' of the movement of the horse under our seat and legs we will know the precise moment when each of the hindlegs is coming to the ground. Therefore, if we apply our left leg just prior to the corresponding hindleg of the horse touching down, the effect will cause that leg to be engaged further under the body and to increase its propulsive thrust. A corresponding action taken by the rider's right leg has the same result on the opposite hindleg and we shall have created more energy and engagement in the hindquarters. Should the hands follow the movement of the head the stride becomes longer and more active. If we simultaneously act in the same fashion with our hands, the left hand closing, and resisting, as the left leg acts and then the right, being operated in the same way as the right leg is applied, we shall retain the activity whilst compressing the horse towards his centre, shifting a little more of the weight to the rear. We are preparing or positioning him in the most effective attitude to pass into trot when our hands yield a little and both our legs act in concert.

It may sound to be a rather complicated way of obtaining so simple a transition as that from walk to trot, but it makes for accuracy and there is no risk of confusing the horse. The reason I prefer the system of the hands resisting alternately is that it avoids creating a base of resistance within the horse's mouth, or, at least, it halves that base. The simultaneous use of both hands provides just such a base, whilst the operation of alternate pressures of minimal duration gives the horse no chance to resist the action. He yields almost without knowing that he does so, the bit gliding across the mouth, applying intermittent pressure alternately on the two sides. Describing this to one young lady I was told this was known as 'sawing' the mouth and was most reprehensible, as any member of the Pony Club holding his or her 'B' test certificate would know. Well, of course, this rippling of the bit on the bars is something very far removed from 'sawing' and if it is a practice not widely known or in general use that is no good reason to condemn it.

For those who find it difficult to know the position at a given moment of the hindlegs, the feel can be developed in quite a short time if you ride round an arena getting someone to count 'Now – now – now – now', each time the inside hind is about to come to the ground. In fact this means that the caller must say 'Now' as the leg is taken off the ground and is beginning to reach forward, otherwise it will be too late. Carry out the exercise on both reins, applying the legs accordingly, until the rhythm is firmly in your mind, then begin the calling yourself in unison with your helper. As the 'feel' develops you will find you will be able to dispense with your caller and with a little practice will be able to apply first your legs and then both legs and hands almost unconsciously. Again, this may be something which you feel is unnecessary and unnecessarily difficult, but aids, though applied according to the book, are pretty useless unless they are applied at exactly the right time and at exactly the point where the horse is best positioned to respond to them correctly. The development of 'feel' in the rider is an absolute essential.

To school horses you must be able to gauge the precise moment at which the application of an aid is likely to achieve a successful result. It is impossible to regard the aids as being able to be given mechanically. To drive a car competently you have to give 'the aids' unconsciously; you change gear, brake or use the wheel without looking at the gear-lever, pedals or wheel and you do so as an automatic reflex, not as a conscious action. Exactly the same holds good for the riding aids but, in fact, I wonder how many average riders ever reach that desirable state. A great many, I fear, remain for ever in the position of the learner car drive who must need to look at the pedals to see where his feet are going and make a conscious effort to co-ordinate his movements. It is rather more difficult on a horse, admittedly, since so much more is involved, but the ability to use *one* leg or *one* hand without its corresponding member acting in sympathy can be achieved if we are prepared to devote sufficient time to intelligent practice.

In making turns the preparation, or pre-positioning of the horse is just as important, and in this phase we should take particular care to ride well into the corners of the school with the horse bent in the direction of the movement. In order to do so, we must warn our horse of the intended turn even though the approaching corner may seem extraordinarily obvious. Prior to reaching the corner our horse must be 'positioned' in readiness. This entails our beginning to bend him very slightly in the direction of the turn about two-thirds down the long side of the school. In this position he is then half-way to making the turn correctly as he enters the corner. If the aids are left to the last moment, i.e. when we are in the corner, the horse just isn't given time to execute the arc correctly and we, in our anxiety, may overdo the acting hand and cause the head to be pulled too much to the inside. By doing so we unbalance our horse and make it impossible for the hindlegs to follow the track of the front pair.

In our schooling sessions we must also include our neck-stretching exercises, allowing our horse to walk and then to trot on a long rein without our losing contact with his mouth. As he is now quite unperturbed by the presence of a low cavalletto we can include one or two in the neck-stretching exercises, crossing them first at walk and then at trot with the rein held long as before. At walk this is easy enough, but it requires a little more skill at trot if we are to maintain the contact on a long rein. The secret is to sit in the saddle for the two strides preceding the cavalletto and to make no undue effort to move our body forward (as we would when jumping) beyond a slight forward inclination of the shoulders. Keep the seat in the saddle with the body relatively upright and allow the small of the back to absorb and follow the movement.

The value of this little exercise, which can be extended by adding up to four cavalletti (between 4 and 6 feet apart according to the stride of our horse) to form a grid, is to increase the engagement of the hocks and to confirm the rounded top-

29 A good jump, maintaining the rounded form, over a cavalletti

30 First steps in teaching the horse to stretch his neck and seek out contact with the bit

line, as well as improving the balance and acting as a strengthening exercise. The head and neck, however, must be down and stretched forward, the nose leading and not being tucked in, and the mouth seeking the contact of the bit.

Making use of the cavalletti again, we can now carry out some of the more elementary mounted jumping work we have done on the lunge. Although our horse has been jumping

147

small fences both loose and on the end of the lunge-line our first efforts at mounted jumping should be confined to the cavalletti grid. The first jump the horse made on the lunge followed the grid exercises, and it was made by moving the third cavalletto and placing it on top of the fourth, the grid being laid at the trotting distance of between 4 and 6 feet. The same procedure must therefore be followed as we introduce him to jumping with a rider on his back. Cross the first two cavalletti at trot with the body inclined slightly forward, the legs in contact and acting with the hands allowing for the head and neck to stretch. If the impulsion is maintained the horse will hop over the little fence with no trouble at all. Should he break into a stride of canter on landing, don't worry, just bring him gently back to trot and then make much of him. The little fence can be jumped up to three times during the schooling session, but between each jump it is advisable to spend a few moments performing simple school figures at walk and trot, so that we avoid any possibility of excitement. The grid must be organized so that it is jumped from both reins, and as the work progresses it can be moved away from the sides of the arena into the centre. Towards the end of this stage vary the exercise by removing the second cavalletto so that the remaining one is 18 feet in front of the fence, and, as before, jump from trot. Although jumping on the lunge and loose will continue over more varied fences during this stage the jumping exercise under saddle as described are sufficient for the moment.

Finally, in the school work, as well as when riding outside, pay particular attention to riding on the correct diagonal at trot.

Hacking and Outside Work

Outside the school the exercise periods cover much the same ground as before and with the same objectives in mind. We want to relax our horse, improve his balance by making use of undulating country and keep him interested. In this stage we can begin to teach him to canter more correctly, striking off with the proper lead as requested, and we can do quite a lot more with his traffic training.

Let us take the canter first. So far the youngster has cantered on the lunge and we have allowed him to lollop along in that pace whilst hacking. We have not, however, asked him to canter a circle under the rider, and particularly not in the confined area of the school, since he will not yet be sufficiently balanced for the exercise. So far, in fact, he has done nothing more than learn a little about how to carry weight at this pace, and we have not been bothered about him striking off on one leg or the other. But on the lunge he has been positioned to strike off correctly and so we have laid a foundation for teaching the canter aids. We can now carry this a stage further when we are hacking.

According to the books the correct aids for canter are inside rein and outside leg, diagonal aids, in fact. Therefore if we apply – as we are circling left – our inside hand and our outside leg the horse should go into canter leading with his left foreleg. But he won't, until he is taught the meaning of those signals – they are quite incomprehensible to him. Furthermore, he has to be correctly positioned and prepared before he is physically able to respond to those aids.

In teaching the canter therefore we must do so step by step. First the horse must learn to carry weight at the pace, and since this is the object it doesn't matter from what aids he is induced to enter the canter. So far we have only pushed him forward energetically until he *fell* into canter. Secondly, he must learn something about striking off on the correct leg from his work on the lunge where his balance is not hampered by the rider's weight, and thirdly we must begin to teach him to canter on a given leg under the rider. The final stage is to gain a smooth departure, on either leg, from the lightest of *diagonal* aids.

Since the diagonal aid is too difficult for him at this point we must approach it by more readily understood indications.

We could make a start on the canter departs in the school making use of our cavalletto across the corner, as we did on the lunge to induce a strike-off with the inside foreleg leading. But the school is too cramped for a youngster with a rider on his back and it is better if he learns to canter in a large area, where he is not constrained to carry himself round the relatively tight corners of the school, something which at this stage increases his difficulties enormously.

Start, therefore, in a fairly large field riding a large circle at trot on whichever rein you like. Ride into one of the corners, marking in your mind a particular spot at which you want to make the depart into canter; well before the place is reached, bring your horse together and ride strongly on; a few paces before the mark sit down in the saddle, holding the body upright, and then apply *lateral* aids. That entails raising your hands a little and carrying them over to the *outside* (right if you are on the circle left). The horse's head will then be inclined to the outside, away from the directional movement, and simultaneously we apply the outside (right in this instance) leg more strongly than its partner and somewhat behind the girth. The effect is to upset the balance of the horse whilst freeing the inside shoulder and asking, by the use of our right leg, for a greater thrust from the right hindleg of the horse, which is the first limb concerned in the three movements leading to canter on the left foreleg. The result, despite the heresy of a lateral aid, is for the horse to fall into canter on the correct leading foreleg, which is what was required. Immediately the foreleg commences the stride, the third sequence in the canter depart (on canter left the sequence is right hind – right diagonal – left fore), straighten the head and ride straight ahead.

Admittedly the performance is not a polished one or even pretty to watch but a result is achieved, and that is important.

It is a relatively simple matter, when the horse is confirmed in correct strike-offs on either leg and is able to canter a large circle to either hand to straighten him gradually until he strikes off from the more orthodox diagonal aid. Whilst it is desirable, indeed essential, that the trained, supple horse (for reasons already given) should always be bent in the direction of the movement we should recognize that in freedom the young horse will frequently canter with his head held to the outside, away from the movement, and this is particularly noticeable when he makes sharp turns. By doing so he frees his inside shoulder and so makes it easier for himself – and that is just what we are doing in this instance. Indeed, very much later on, if we take up show-jumping seriously, we may well have to resort to this little trick of turning the head away from the movement when we are faced with making an exceptionally tight turn at speed.

Having achieved a canter, do not let it become a mad gallop but keep the horse going quietly within himself and don't be frightened of cantering on gently for as much as half a mile or so. So many horses have difficulties with cantering and even more become impossibly excited solely for the reason that they do not get enough practice at the pace. Provided the horse is fairly fit and not carrying too much fat and the ground is not excessively hard work at canter – within reason – will do him no harm and will assist in the development of balance.

Riding in Traffic

Whilst hacking across country it is now reasonable, at least towards the end of this stage, to expect our youngster to go out unaccompanied, but it is still advisable to have the company of an older horse when riding in traffic.

Road work, which besides accustoming the horse to traffic is a means of hardening his legs, should be done at the second session of the day when the horse has already got some work under his belt.

Up to now we have used the older horse to give a lead and to act as a shield against the traffic, positioning him accordingly. If our youngster seems to be quite equable about the

normal road hazards we should now begin to reduce his reliance upon the older horse. To commence, let the pupil still
be ridden on the inside of his companion but gradually encourage him – on a suitable piece of quiet road, where one can
see for some distance – to take the lead by about a neck's distance as a vehicle approaches from the front, whilst still remaining on the inside of the schoolmaster horse. By degrees
the distance can be increased until the two horses are in single
file. In the same way let him drop to the rear as a car approaches from behind until the same result is achieved.

I am firmly of the opinion that half the battle in traffic training depends on the intelligent anticipation of the rider. Indeed, riding depends on that factor all the time, whether in
traffic or not. A rider who is alert and constantly riding mentally a good 100 yards in front and behind him when on the
road, will rarely get into trouble. Roads today are not places
where one can admire the scenery and lollop along on a loose
rein. On any horse, particularly a young one, you must *ride*
every inch of the way.

A greater part of the remaining half of the battle, which is
again equally applicable to riding elsewhere, lies in the correct
positioning of the horse. There is a school of thought which
holds that it is better to turn the horse's head away from approaching traffic but it is not one to which I could logically
subscribe. If the turning of the head away from the traffic is
supposed to prevent him seeing it, the argument holds no
water at all, since the position of the horses' eyes is such that
he has considerable side-vision. What is more, by bending the
head to the left (given that we are riding on the left of the road)
we position the horse to swing his quarters to the opposite
direction and, should he be startled, his quarters are likely to
spin out right into the path of the approaching car.

If our horse is obedient to the aids (and no horse should be
ridden in traffic on his own until he is), the logical thing to do
is to incline the head slightly towards the vehicle and apply the
right leg on the girth using the left leg in support. Now, he is
positioned so that it is difficult for him to evade our aids, and
should he swing his quarters it will be into the hedge and not
into the car.

At this point our young horse is not sufficiently experienced
to go out on his own nor is he sufficiently educated in his responses to the aids. By the end of his schooling period, if we
have taught him his lessons properly, he will be safe to ride on
the road, because such will be his trust in us and so deeply
rooted will be the habit of obedience that he will obey even
when frightened.

During this period of training every advantage should be
taken of opportunities to attend small shows even though the

horse competes in nothing at all. Riding him round with other horses present and letting him see and hear unusual sights and sounds is all part of his education and provides a change from his ordinary work.

Duration of Stages 1 and 2

Exactly how long should be spent on these two stages is once more dependent upon the progress the horse makes in his work, his physical condition and his mental outlook. However, it is most important that it should not be hurried since this is a period primarily devoted to recapitulation of the work done in the previous year and to the improvement of his physique. In general, it is unlikely to be completed in under eight to ten weeks, which takes us into around mid-June if we have started early in April.

The work and exercise can be divided into two periods a day as before, with the horse being allowed to graze at liberty and to relax for an hour or two each day.

Lungeing and loose schooling at the end of the period can be increased up to twenty to thirty minutes per day, ridden schooling in the menage to twenty minutes or so, each with frequent short periods of rest, and hacking exercise may be as much as one and a quarter hours each day.

Physical Condition

As in every preceding stage, the horse should be examined daily for any sign of strain or injury. Constant attention should be given to the teeth and worming should be carried out regularly according to veterinary advice. It is particularly important that the horse should be wormed at the outset of the second phase of training and that a veterinary surgeon should examine his teeth. The horse will still be in the process of shedding teeth and may experience discomfort when doing so. Should this occur, there is no point in exacerbating the condition and risking the possibility of creating an habitual resistance in the mouth by continuing to ride him. It is much better to be patient and cut out the ridden work for a day or so.

Although most of the jumping work in the first two stages is unmounted, this is a dangerous time in the development of the young horse as far as splints are concerned, and it is stupid to continue the jumping exercises if the going becomes very hard, when the jar experienced on landing will be more accentuated. In any case, continue to use protective boots when schooling. Above all, do not allow your young horse to become fat. Overweight puts additional burdens on the legs and the internal organs.

Chapter 15   Phase 2 : Stage 3

In the next stages we continue working towards the creation of what I have termed the 'whole' horse, increasing the lateral and longitudinal suppleness and improving the effective balance. As a result our horse will become ready at last to take on a higher head-carriage, from which we shall start to obtain greater lightness in front and increased obedience to the hand.

In fact we are aiming for greater control over our horse and his movements, which will be made possible by his increased physical ability and improved balance.

We shall still, however, make use of the lunge as a preparation for ridden work and jumping and we shall extend the loose schooling exercises, making use (if we can find or make one) of a jumping lane.

As previously, we will deal with the work involved under the headings of Lunge Work and Loose Schooling, Ridden Work and Hacking.

Lunge Work

On the lunge we now begin to ask for greater perfection in the movement, especially the maintenance of even rhythm and correct lateral bends.

At trot, still using the now shortened side-reins we can increase the lateral suppleness by alternately reducing and enlarging the size of the circle, whilst maintaining a steady rhythm. Of course, this work must only be of short duration, since long periods would cause the horse discomfort and could result in a shortening of the stride. Do not be afraid of asking the head to turn inwards by giving little jerks on the cavesson, but on the other hand, do not ask for too great a bend; it must be uniform from poll to tail. Five minutes of this exercise in any one session is sufficient, if well done.

The exercise will reveal the 'stiff' side of the horse just as surely as when he is worked under saddle. Theoretically as we should have been working more on the side to which the horse bends with less facility throughout the training, there should not be a 'stiff' side at this stage, but in practice it is usually there to some degree. More frequently than otherwise the horse will be naturally more stiff when circling to the right, but the opposite may also occur. It will be necessary therefore to do more work on the 'stiff' side than on the other and this will also apply when we use the long lunge line off the bit in the advanced form of lungeing aimed at putting the horse on the hand. If the horse is very stiff (which he should not be) it may be necessary to use the second method (see Figure 23) in this work, but usually this is reserved for the older horse in need of correction.

The third method may, however, be used beneficially if the horse tends to overbend towards the centre, evading the bend of the whole body by falling in towards the trainer. This, indeed, is quite likely to happen when the circle is reduced in size.

The work on the long lunge line from the bit, and without, of course, the side-reins, should form a regular part of the lungeing sessions and may be used at canter as well as at trot once we have perfected the former pace on the cavesson.

Cantering on the Lunge

The horse has already been prepared for cantering on the lunge by the use of the cavalletto across the corner, inducing him to strike off correctly, and by cantering for a few strides on elements of a circle. Now he should be ready to canter a full circle on the lunge, and it is certain that until he can do this without difficulty he will be unable to perform a similar figure under saddle.

But, of course, it must be approached gradually, asking a little more each day as the horse's physique and balance improve. Always commence on a large circle and do not be afraid to move with the horse to allow him greater freedom if it is felt that the circle is too small. Having got the horse cantering a circle on both reins (with the side-reins adjusted a little longer to accord with the pace) we can concentrate on the strike-off and the rhythm, reducing the diameter of the circle. But before doing so, be quite sure that the horse is quite comfortable on the circle. Ideally, he should virtually carry the rein himself. If there is a continued tendency for him to hang against the hand then the circle is too small for him and you are expecting too much too soon.

It will, in fact, take some weeks before we can really begin on the refinements, the first of which is the **Strike-Off**.

Prior to putting the horse into canter the trot needs to be shortened by the use of hand and voice but without loss of impulsion. The bend should then be made more definite by a quick increase of tension on the rein to *position* the horse in the correct attitude. Immediately following this movement the hand (and, therefore, the head) can be raised, the rein then being carried out to the side at the moment the command **Canter** is given, to lead the horse into the first stride. It should only be necessary to make a slow, momentary sweep with the whip as the command is given. A sudden, violent movement of the whip only distracts the horse and may frighten him, so that he upsets his balance in a quick movement to get away from the threatening thong. It is easier at first to get a smooth, relaxed strike-off if the trainer stands fairly close to the horse, from which position he can exert the maximum control. However, whilst standing close is easier, it means that the rein must be let out immediately the sequence of canter footfalls commences, i.e. on the strike-off of the outside hindleg. If you are later than this in releasing the rein, the first stride of canter will be restricted by the tension on the cavesson causing too great an inward bend of the head.

To start with, most horses will set off too fast. We really want, as an ideal, a change of gait without any alteration in the speed. Initially, this is again best obtained by the trainer working close to his horse, checking him gently, as soon as the canter is established, with his voice and rein, and yet being able from this position to prevent a falling-back into trot. Obviously this entails considerable movement on the trainer's part until such time as he can obtain the gait without moving from his central position. Incidentally, when one has to move in this fashion inside a cantering horse it is easier to move in a sideways canter rhythm oneself, leading with one's left leg on the circle left, and vice-versa, and then bringing the other leg up to the leading one without crossing it over its partner. It may look a little silly, but the horse won't mind.

This work from the cavesson and the bit will take up most of the lunge session, in which periods of rest must be frequent. Even so, as a change for the horse, he should continue to do a few moments' work over the grid and perhaps over one or two small fences of the kind described.

Loose Schooling

Once a week during this stage the horse can school loose over fences, and, whilst we can carry this out fairly satisfactorily in the school, it has to be admitted that much of the trainer's attention is given to positioning and controlling the horse. It is, of course, an excellent lesson in obedience but if we can make use of a jumping lane (of the sort illustrated) it is undoubtedly easier to concentrate on the actual jump and it will also enable us, because of its shape, to make use of fences in combinations down the long sides. For this last reason an oval

31 Mounted work in the jumping
lane

shape is to be preferred approximating to the dimensions given in Figure 13 (p. 57). A jumping lane set in a straight line is not so good, since it encourages a horse to rush his fences.

To build a first-class lane is a matter of some expense, but quite a good one can be built without it costing too much. However, should you be in funds, build your lane as in Figure 13 with the enclosure being a good 5 feet in height and the outer one fitted with a hurdle screen to prevent the horse being distracted by what goes on outside. Fences can be virtually fixed, and all that is needed for their construction is a supply of really stout poles plus bales or drums to add variety. Absolutely fixed fences are not really very kind, since a mistake by the horse can punish him too severely and may shake his confidence. If the type of stand illustrated is used and the poles placed carefully in the centre, there is a play of some 4 inches on each side, which is enough to inspire respect without causing a fall. In this type of lane it is possible to put either two or four fences; initially those on the short sides being there to discourage any tendency to rush. Later on, the long sides can be made to take a combination with either 24 feet (one non-jumping stride) or 33 feet (two non-jumping strides) between them.

Two fences are sufficient to start with, one an upright with a ground pole placed in front of it to make judgement of the take-off easier and the other a parallel. In time, the fences can be raised up to 3 feet 6 inches or even 4 feet, but for the moment 2 feet 6 inches to 3 feet is sufficient for the upright, with the ground pole being placed the same distance away in front, whilst the spread need not exceed 2 feet 6 inches × 2 feet 6 inches. If the anti-rush fences are needed, a 2 foot pole will suffice. The beauty of this type of jumping lane is that it allows the horse to be worked by one person. On the first occasions it will be necessary to follow the horse round the track, but thereafter he can be sent off and the trainer can move round the central oval controlling the horse with voice and whip.

Certain vague evils are attributed to loose schooling but none, as far as I can discover, are very relevant. The most specific argument I have heard against the use of a jumping lane is that it will teach a horse to jump out of his field. If that is true why teach the horse to jump at all? In my experience animals that jump out of fields do so whether they have been loose-schooled or not.

On the other hand, jumping in complete freedom without the weight of the rider improves the horse's judgement of stride, distance and approach, builds up his confidence and develops his *initiative*. Indeed, horses so schooled rarely jump in anything but good style and form. It is the unschooled, or improperly schooled, horse that jumps flat with a hollow back.

Jumping in good rounded form, the horse arching in line with the parabola of the leap, is not just an aesthetic pleasure but a very practical aspect of jumping. Not only does the horse jump cleanly over the obstacle but the very act of rounding impels him to raise up both hind- and forelegs. For the expenditure of the same effort a schooled horse makes a bigger jump than the one who jumps flat with legs trailing.

A certain show-jumping element would say that they do not require a horse to think or show initiative, preferring to 'place' the horse themselves and demanding complete obedience to their aids. The majority, however, would agree that a certain initiative is desirable and on many occasions can be most helpful.

Ridden Schooling

So far our ridden work has been concerned with:

1 Teaching the horse to carry and accept weight.
2 Improving his balance and paces under weight.
3 Teaching him to move forward from the legs to *seek* out and accept the bit.
4 Lateral suppling and the beginning of longitudinal suppling.

In this stage, and in those that follow, we begin to build on those carefully prepared foundations. Already we should have fulfilled the first requirement of *Calm* and we have gone quite a long way to ensure obedience to the second, our horse going **Forward** willingly. Now we must work *towards* the completion of General L'Hotte's trinity and get our horse **Straight**.

The suppling work we have already done goes some way towards straightness, but there is still a long path to tread before we can claim to have a **Straight** horse, and indeed, we are unlikely to achieve that quality in its entirety within this second phase.

Similarly, whilst our work has contributed to a higher natural carriage of head and neck brought about by our horse's increased engagement of his quarters, we have not been specifically concerned with this aspect. From this point, we become increasingly concerned, since without the *naturally* high carriage it will be difficult for us to improve the lightness of forehand *and* quarters and consequently bring his state of balance to a higher level.

To achieve this more elevated head-carriage the lateral and longitudinal suppleness of our horse must be increased by rather more demanding exercises, which in this stage will not be beyond the physical capacity of our pupil.

1 **Lateral Suppling** As a prelude to these exercises we return to those involving the stretching of the neck, but in a more advanced form. We employ a technique known as 'combing' the rein, in order to induce an even greater stretch of the neck and its muscles. The object is to continue the build-up of muscle on the top-line of the neck and to obviate by this means any possibility of producing a neck which falls in the front of the withers, causing it to look like the spout of a tea-pot. A neck so carried does not induce a tension in the back and the accompanying engagement of the quarters.

Commencing at walk, the rider first transfers the reins to one hand held at the withers. The other hand holds the buckle end of the reins at chest level. The rein hand is held palm-down with the reins between the fingers and is then allowed to slide upwards to take the place of the other hand, which is then moved above the wither to commence the exercise again. The hands continue to act in this fashion whilst the legs maintain the impulsion. In a few ten-minute lessons the horse will begin to stretch his neck, and in a similar time, the average rider will acquire the necessary knack of manipulating the hands smoothly without losing contact. The exercise carried out at the beginning of each lesson, and with another five minutes half-way through devoted to stretching and relaxing the neck in this manner, will make all the difference to the performance of the ensuing exercise. The stretching of muscles

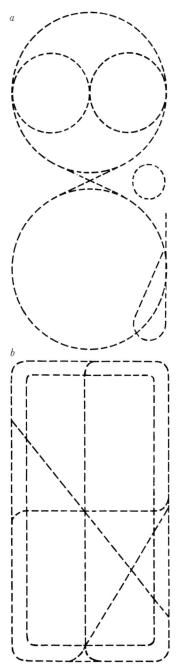

Figure 25
Some of the ridden school figures designed to supple the horse.
(*a*) circles and changes of hand.
(*b*) The various changes of hand possible in a school area. The inside dotted line indicates the 'inside' track, i.e. 6 ft from the wall.

is followed by their relaxation, and when the muscles relax, the head is necessarily lowered. Until we can obtain this relaxation, we cannot ask for the contraction of the muscles required in a higher carriage.

Following the stretching exercise, the reins can be picked up, the horse pushed well up to his bridle and we can begin riding simple figures, gradually working up to serpentines and then at first fairly large and then much smaller circles to either hand, but putting the emphasis on the 'stiff' side. As the muscles on each side of the horse are stretched alternately in the curves required by the serpentine, a definite relaxation of the mouth on the inside rein will become apparent. Since it follows that the greater the degree of the curve taken by the horse's body, the greater will be the extent to which the muscles are stretched, the changes of direction imposed by the serpentine and the smaller circles are ideal for this suppling exercise. In the early stages, however, the horse may need to be put into the required curve by fairly strong actions of the legs and even of the spur. The exercises, when carried out at trot after commencing at walk, will probably be made easier if the rider *sits* at that pace. So far the use of the *sitting trot* has been minimal for the reason that if it were to be employed before the back was sufficiently strong and muscled and had acquired a tension it would have prevented the round form and the engaged quarters. By this time, however, our horse will be quite capable of carrying us in this position, in which our aids, including our weight and seat, can be employed with greater effect.

2 **Longitudinal Suppling** exercises are carried out concurrently with the preceding ones and begin with increases and decreases of the pace at walk. From the extended walk the reins are taken up and the outline shortened by alternate legs pushing the horse on to resisting fingers, as was explained in a previous stage (p. 113).

At the trot the slow-downs and speed-ups are of greater value. With the rising trot well established, the rider begins the resistance with the fingers then assumes the sitting position using both legs to drive the horse into the resistance of the hands. Again, it is probably advisable to use the hands alternately, the resistance of one following immediately upon the other, rather than to encourage a similar resistance in the mouth by using the hands simultaneously. At first, a few strides in the shortened posture is sufficient, and then the fingers should cease their resistance and the horse be allowed to stretch onwards with the rider rising once more. As the horse becomes more proficient and the shortening and extension more defined, the speed-ups and slow-downs can be

SERPENTINE

SPIRAL

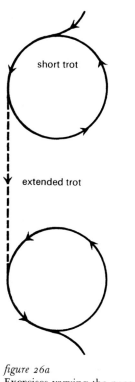

short trot

extended trot

short trot

figure 26a
Exercises varying the pace at trot canter.

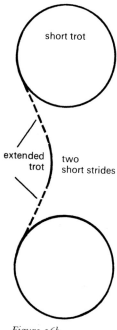

short trot

extended trot

two short strides

Figure 26b

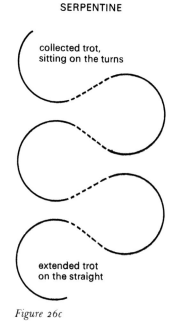

collected trot, sitting on the turns

extended trot on the straight

Figure 26c

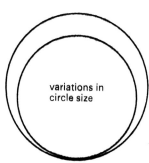

variations in circle size

Figure 26d

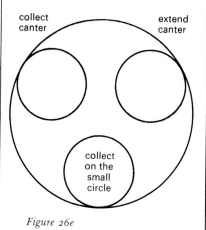

collect canter

extend canter

collect on the small circle

Figure 26e

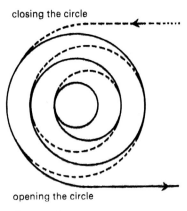

closing the circle

opening the circle

Figure 26f

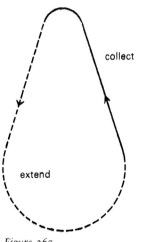

collect

extend

Figure 26g

performed across the diagonal of the schooling area and then in the corners. Initially, the horse can be shortened entering the corner (when both lateral and longitudinal suppling will be effected) and extended down the long sides, and then the exercise can be reversed. A variety of similar exercises can be ridden as are shown in Figures 25 and 26. Transitions from one pace to another including halt (which at this stage, whilst we have yet to supple *each* of the hindlegs, may not be entirely square) will also encourage longitudinal suppleness and improve the balance by the shifting of weight entailed.

Over a period of weeks the head will begin to take a more elevated attitude and there will be a subsequent lightening of the forehand. However, this must be brought about by the engagement of the back-end under the body and any temptation to niggle the head into a better position with the hands has to be resisted.

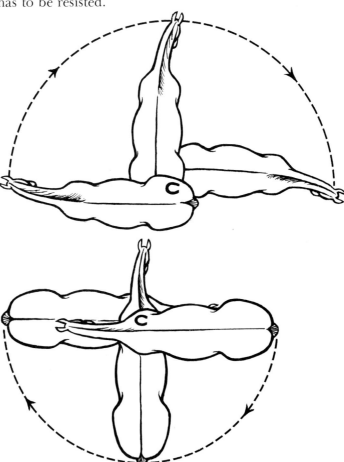

Figure 27
The half-turn on the quarters.

Figure 28
The half-turn on the forehand.

Once the head is coming up and the horse is experiencing no difficulty with these exercises we can turn our attention to lightening **Both Ends**, which is best reached by first improving

the **Mobility of the Quarters**. As a start, we shall teach our
horse to move his quarters laterally, away from the action of
a single leg, and finally, although not in this stage, to move his
quarters round his forelegs in a *turn on the forehand*.

This turn and the other, the *turn on the haunches* (which is
taught later on) is a prime example of man improving on
nature since neither are performed in freedom, or rarely at
any rate. A frightened horse may very occasionally turn on his
quarters but never on his forehand. The natural turn is that
of all four legs round the vertical axis at the girth, the same,
in fact, as we have been practising in our school work so far.
It could be argued that very little of the horse's training is
natural, but, with the exception of jumping, it is all very much
nearer to the natural movements than the work upon which
we shall now embark. These movements mark the watershed between the partially schooled horse and the trained
one, who is so much more responsive and under far greater
control.

Now that is the sort of cut-and-dried statement which, if it
was addressed to me, would immediately prompt the question, 'Yes, that may well be, but why is the horse any better for
being taught to move his quarters this way and that?' It probably provoked the same reaction in many of you, too. The
answer is, that by teaching the horse to move his quarters from
the single leg aid we cause a crossing of the hindlegs and we
are therefore given a means of strengthening and suppling
each hindleg individually. This must increase the efficiency of
the horse and must therefore be beneficial.

Secondly, by having the ability to move the quarters with
our legs at will, it follows that we also have the ability to
correct any unwanted shift of that end. Now that means we
are approaching the 'straight' horse. In fact, there is much
more to it than that, because it is **Only When We Can Control
the Quarters That We Can Control the Horse!**

Most of us, possibly because we sit on a horse facing the
front and in our first riding lessons control our horses entirely
from that end, associate the majority of resistances with the
head and neck. If our horse goes left when we want him to go
right we instinctively pull the right rein or, at least, as beginners we do. Well, of course, there are resistances made in
the mouth but the great source of resistance is not at that end
at all but behind the saddle, in the quarters, since it is they
which initiate movement and changes of direction not the
head! Let us be quite clear that all turns are initiated by the
quarters, the head and neck only *indicate* the turn. They are not
connected directly to the quarters and so, even though the
head and neck are inclined to the right you will still go to the
left, if that is the direction of the drive made by the quarters

(unless, of course, you can position the quarters in the direction you require them to take by means of your legs).

The quarters are in fact connected to the **Shoulders**, the balancing and lightening of which will be discussed in due course. Because this is so, it is possible to place the shoulders in front and in line with the drive of the quarters. But you can't put the driving quarters, the originators of the movement, behind the shoulders, which have little to do with it. Therefore, we must be able to control the drive of the quarters and, if we cannot control them, then we cannot hope to eradicate the resistance which arise in them.

We must ride from *rear* to *front*, thinking of the quarters as a rudder rather than the mouth as a steering wheel. First place the quarters then adjust the head accordingly. Unless we can grasp this essential truth, even if it does turn all our ideas about riding upside down, then we cannot go further in the training of the horse.

Heaviness in front is the result of resistance in the quarters and an inability to control them, particularly when making changes of direction. If we make a turn by the forehand alone, pulling it over in the direction required, which is what we were doing with the direct, opening rein in the very early stages, we can get round the corner, but at the expense of lightness in front. The forehand turns, but the quarters can continue in their original direction. We may get away with it in part by attempting to bend the horse round our inside leg, but very little real flexion is achieved until the quarters are under control. As another example, think of the horse who runs out at a fence, whilst all the time his rider is endeavouring to put him straight with the rein. The root of the trouble is an unwanted shift of the quarters driving the horse away from the fence. If we can control the quarters that unwanted shift could have been corrected almost before it got under-way and we should have avoided a run out.

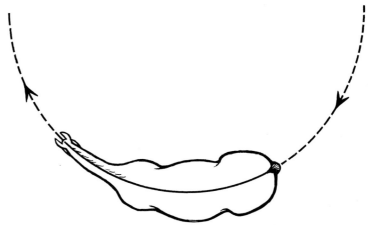

Figure 29
The true bend on the circle, the horse bent uniformly from poll to tail.

Finally, until we obtain lateral mobility in the quarters in answer to the single leg, we cannot hold them for correctly executed turns on the haunches, circles, voltes, serpentines, etc. Once more, **Only When We Can Control the Quarters Can We Control the Horse**.

Having made the point as emphatically as I am able, let us consider the method of teaching this desirable control over the quarters.

There is one famous book on riding which advocates the turn on the forehand being taught from the saddle, the horse being halted against the wall and then constrained by a pushing leg to turn his back-end round his forehand. It sounds delightfully simple until you try it, although I am sure it was all perfectly straightforward for the gifted horseman–author – whom, I suspect, omitted to inform his readers of the preparations leading up to the manoeuvre. Anyway, it is too difficult for me, and so I must work up to the ultimate turn on the forehand by easy stages.

In a small way we have been preparing our horse to yield his quarters by tapping them over to both sides in the box, and the first lessons in the school will therefore be a follow-on from this very elementary training.

The first step is for the trainer to stand slightly to the side of the horse's head facing the tail. He then leads the horse forward whilst he keeps his position and walks backwards, holding the bridle in one hand, some six inches from the bit. When the horse is walking out freely he must then slow him down slightly, incline the head just a little towards him – which facilitates a shift of the quarters in the opposite direction – then tap the horse low down behind the girth with the long whip. Inevitably, the horse will move away from the whip and he may possibly cross his hindlegs once or even twice, which is very good. The moment he does so, walk him forward in the new line dictated by the position of the quarters and make much of him. Don't prolong the lesson but be satisfied if you get the legs to cross once. The mistake to avoid is that of inclining the head too much, which will cause the horse to spin round and virtually come to a stop. For those who may be wondering why the exercise is not done at halt but at walk, it is because we do not wish to stop the horse going **Forward**. In this, as in everything we do, forward movement is paramount. The horse must always maintain this urge to go forward, even indeed, when later on he reins back! In this instance, loss of forward movement would be fatal, since the object is to control the horse's quarters in movement and not solely when they are at halt. The turn on the forehand is in itself only a means to an end, although it may have certain practical applications. Furthermore, teaching the turn from

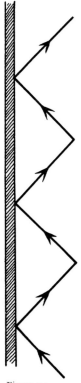

Figure 30
The zig-zag. A useful figure to ride when teaching obedience to the action of the single leg.

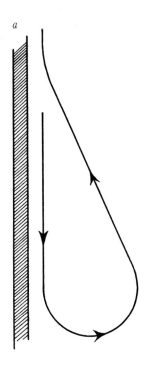

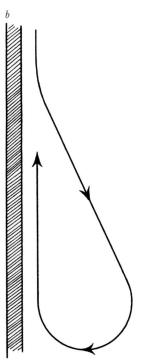

Figure 31
(a) The half-volte, from which figure is taught the turn on the quarters.
(b) The reverse half-volte, from which is taught the forehand turn.

halt will virtually eliminate the marking-time movement of the outside foreleg, itself a result of forward movement, which is a feature of the complete forehand turn.

If the exercise is practised for five minutes a day it should not take more than ten days or so before the horse is able to cross his hindlegs once in both directions. We can then begin to teach the same thing from the saddle whilst still practising the movement on foot to improve its quality and increase the number of crossings made.

In the saddle we follow much the same procedure, slowing down the walk before using the rein to turn the head very slightly. If we wish then to move the quarters to the left (having positioned the head oppositely) we maintain the impulsion with our left leg acting lightly on the girth (from rear to front) whilst our right moves from *front* to *rear* and slightly further back (now you understand the insistence on the leg aids being made crystal-clear from the beginning). Initially, we shall have to use the long whip to reinforce the request of the right leg and inevitably we shall find movement to one side is more difficult than to the other. Consequently, it will be that side which receives more of our attention.

When we can achieve an easy shift to both sides we can take the next step and ride a zig-zag down the school, using the same aids to make the changes of direction. From here we proceed to the next exercise, the riding of the *reversed half-volte* which will lead us up to the final forehand turn. This is made, as in Figure 31, by leaving the track on an oblique line and returning to it by a small (six-metre) half circle.

To begin with, the horse can be accustomed to the exercise by performing it at walk without any attempt being made to shift the quarters. Then we can go a stage further and complete the circle in the quarters-out position. The way to do this is to place the forehand on the circle, using (if we follow the direction shown in Figure 31) the right direct rein of opposition, which, you will remember, has the effect of pushing the quarters to the left. Slow the horse down as the forehand is placed on the half-circle and, as the check is made and the rein applied, act with the right leg moving from *front* to *rear* whilst the left maintains the impulsion by being applied equally from *rear* to *front*. Your weight should be placed on the seatbone nearest to the direction of the movement, in this case the left seatbone, in order to encourage the movement in that direction. The weight is then following the shift of the horse's centre of balance, or perhaps more correctly, it is imposing a movement on that centre. At this stage it is sufficient if the half-circle is completed with the quarters out in this manner. It will not be a turn on the forehand but it will be getting pretty close to one, and as the training progresses, the half-circle can be made smaller until, at last, we obtain a half forehand turn. At least, that is what should happen, but in practice it is not so simple, since to make the forehand turn correctly it will be necessary to employ the classical *diagonal* aids, the ones so far described being *lateral* aids. However, we will deal with those in a moment.

First let us look at the difficulties we are likely to find in applying the simple aids we have been talking about. Once again, even at this fairly elementary level, the application of these aids emphasizes the importance of the rider having learnt his job before attempting to teach the horse. If you think about it, there are a number of physical movements involved here, most of which take place simultaneously. Following the slow-down or check as the forehand is placed on the circle we act with one hand, the other supporting; both legs are active and working in opposite directions, and we need to weight one seatbone, also. All of which entails the use of separate limbs acting in differing ways within a combination of aids. Unless you have learnt to ride you will be in much the same state as the learner-driver at his first lesson, desperately attempting to sort out clutch, brake, accelerator, gear lever and steering wheel.

Then there is also the strength, or measure, of the aids to consider. Usually, since the rider is concentrating hard on the sequence, they will be applied too strongly, and as a result the horse will react in similar fashion or more likely will resist their indications. If the hand is too strong we will stop the movement forwards or, in combination with the legs, achieve only a turn on the horse's centre. Again, the legs must move to exactly the same extent. If the right moves further to the rear than the left moves to the front, the quarters could just swing over too much, particularly if the strength of the right leg is very much greater than that of the left. Oppositely, if the left leg is too strong, no shift of the quarters will be made at all. In practice, a stronger application of the right leg is all right and one is unlikely to have much trouble in this respect.

After the fault of applying the aids too forcefully, the most common errors to be avoided are: (1) leaning back, which overweights the quarters and therefore reduces their mobility and (2) looking down at the active leg asking for the shift (the right in this case). This causes the weight to be put on the corresponding seatbone, a thing which most people will do almost instinctively and something to be guarded against.

To make the complete half-turn on the forehand, which will be reached somewhat later in the training and for which the horse may not be ready until after the completion of this phase, it is necessary to teach the **Second Rein Effect**, which so far we have conveniently ignored.

The second rein effect is used when making a turn with one hand. This is one practical purpose of the rein and, as we have already mentioned, another is when a sharp turn is required at speed. For the moment our use of the rein is as a means to an end. To teach the horse the Second Rein Effect is quite easily accomplished from the simple direct rein. Apply this last rein a few times as you ride into corners, then gradually shift the emphasis from the inside to the outside hand, allowing the latter to be raised and to press the rein against the horse's neck whilst the inside hand is still carried outwards. The result will be for the horse to turn his nose slightly *away* from the movement (to the outside, in fact), thus freeing and lightening the inside shoulder, which will allow the turn to be made possibly more sharply than you expect. Now take the reins in one hand, the outside one (the right hand for riding a left circle, and vice-versa), raise and advance the hand as the corner is entered and carry it to the *inside*, thus laying on the neck rein, and you will make the turn. For this exercise do not worry about the horse poking his nose away from the direction of the turn, it is of no importance in the context of teaching obedience to the rein.

Having taught this rein, which will not take long, we can return to the half-forehand turn and bring it to a successful conclusion.

At this point, you may be wondering what on earth this odd rein action has to do with a turn on the forehand which had been virtually achieved by using the simpler direct rein of opposition, the third effect. Well, in order for the quarters to turn round the front-end it is fairly obvious that the latter must be kept still. In order to achieve this, still remaining with our turn to the right, it is necessary for the shoulders to be prevented from moving to the left. We want to fix the shoulders to provide a point around which the quarters turn. And this is exactly what we can do by using this rein, the effect of which is entirely on the shoulders. It follows that, if by using the rein in this way we can move the shoulders, we can also stop their movement to one side or the other. We fix the shoulders and complete our half-forehand turn in this way.

We begin by reducing the size of the half-circle on our reversed half-volte, gradually slowing down until we are *virtually* at halt. Now we use the indirect rein on the **Left** to keep the forehand in place and prevent the movement of the shoulders to the left. This will place the head slightly to the left. Our legs then act as before, the left to maintain impulsion and the right asking for the shift of the quarters and the crossing of the hindlegs. The half-turn is then made round the inside foreleg, which marks time in the four beat of the walk. Once the turn is accomplished from walk then it may be done at halt, but it is unlikely that this point will be reached in this phase.

Throughout the period in which the horse is being taught to yield his quarters in response to the single leg, it is absolutely essential to practise the movement in both directions, laying greater emphasis on the side to which the horse finds it more difficult.

Preparing to Turn on the Quarters

Before attempting the turn on the quarters which, apart from its practical use, is a means of lightening the forehand by the weight being put to the rear (just as the turn on the forehand lightened the quarters by placing the weight forward) it is necessary to have obtained a naturally high-carriage of the head and neck. It is no good attempting these turns until this requirement has been met, for if the head is too low there will be no lightening effect since it will not be possible for the weight to be moved to the rear – an essential element in executing the turn.

The French call this high carriage *ramener*, and it is defined as the head being close to the vertical with the poll at the apex,

32 The extreme of collection – the 'ramener'

a position brought about by *the advance of the body towards the head*, the body being driven forward on to gently resisting hands. This position is the apogee of our training, and is the reason for the continued insistence on building up the top line, creating the neck of 'tempered steel' with no caving-in in front of the wither.

Achieved correctly, the top line is tautened, the horse is shortened both at the base and the top by the increased engagement of the quarters, and the resultant position of the head permits the bit to act with maximum efficiency upon the bars of the mouth.

Incorrectly obtained, when the position becomes a travesty of *ramener* and the antithesis of training, the result is an over-bent horse not going to the bit but retreating from its action, the fault of reversing the definition of *ramener* and causing the head to be retracted towards the body by the hands. Unfortunately, if not quite to this extreme extent, you will see many examples of head-carriage imposed by hands, as well as by other dark pieces of gadgetry, in the show-ring, the animals moving with caved-in necks, hollow backs and disengaged quarters. The action, in the front, may appear spectacular, but the horse exhibiting it is unlikely to be much good across a country.

If the head is raised excessively by the hands or other means, what happens is that the first of the cervical vertebrae presses down and exerts pressure on the second, and so on, and as a consequence you must get a hollow back obviating maximum thrust from engaged quarters.

33 Extension at the trot

Correctly engaged hindlegs thrust *forward* and *upwards*, with the result that a lightness is obtained in the raised forehand. It is unlikely, again, that we shall as yet achieve an acceptable *ramener*, but this is what we should have in our minds as the final goal.

The Turn on the Quarters

This turn is taught following that on the forehand for the reason that in turning on the quarters our legs must now *resist* to hold those quarters in place, whereas in the forehand turn the leg *acted*. Therefore, until the horse has learnt to shift his quarters from the single leg, it must follow that we cannot oppose an unwanted shift and hold the quarters in the desired position for a turn to be made on them.

By teaching the horse to yield to the leg not only do we make him more sensitive to its action but we provide ourselves with the means by which the horse will respond to a resisting leg.

The turn on the quarters is taught because:

a The source of many resistances is to be found in the quarters, as we have seen, and if we are to eradicate those resistances then we must be able to control the quarters in which they originate. In fact, we must be able to *hold* them with our legs.

b It supples the shoulders just as the forehand turn suppled the hindquarters.

c It rebalances the horse. The forehand ·turn lightened the quarters and now the turn on the quarters lightens the forehand in a similar fashion. Both turns, therefore, contribute to an overall improvement in the balance.

The turn on the quarters is nonetheless the most difficult of the two and calls for an exactitude in the intensity of the leg aid, which is not of such vital importance in the forehand turn. If we acted too strongly with the leg in the forehand turn it would have been possible for the quarters to go over too far but, in general, it would not have been a matter for great concern. However, if we *resist* with our legs too forcefully in this turn it will matter a great deal since it will cause the horse to move his quarters when we want him to keep them still.

We approached the forehand turn from the reversed half-volte and to teach the turn on the quarters we employ the ordinary half-volte made the opposite way round, i.e. leaving the track on a half-circle and returning to it obliquely. If the half-volte is ridden from the left rein as in Figure 31 we make the half-circle gradually smaller with each half-volte that is ridden. When the circle is really quite small, start the exercise

34 A magnificent picture showing an almost perfect turn

35 The half-volte

by checking the horse, then (a) the right leg slides back to keep the quarters *inside* the track of the forelegs which are on the half-circle, and (b) the right indirect rein is applied to shift the shoulders *left*.

The left hand prevents movement to the front, the left leg acts gently on the girth to give a little impulsion and the horse will cross his forelegs once or twice, which is the beginning of the turn.

When this can be done to either hand with equal ease make the circle even smaller, check the walk by putting your own weight to the rear, that is, by allowing the shoulders to move a little behind the line of the hips. This action obviously places more weight on the horse's quarters and so makes a sideways, evading movement more difficult. Additionally, the transference of the rider's weight reduces the burden on the forehand and, thus lightened, it moves with more ease. On the trained horse it will only be necessary to stretch upwards with the back but with the novice the aids need to be slightly exaggerated if they are to achieve their purpose. Eventually, we will be able to execute the turn on the quarters on the spot, but it is too early to attempt it in this stage and phase.

Why do we teach the turn from walk? First, for the very good reason that it is easier for the horse to understand our meaning and execute the movement, and secondly, because we obviate the very present danger of running back when the turn is requested, something most definitely not to be encouraged.

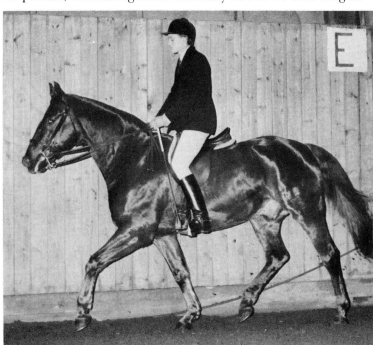

36 The early departures into canter from trotting on the inside diagonal

37 The rider has 'fallen' into the canter pace on the correct inside lead

The difficulty with the leg aids has been mentioned, but the hands have their problems, too. If the rein is too tight the horse goes backwards; if it is too loose he moves forward. The hands must therefore learn to operate with delicacy. Once more no physical strength is required: this will only provoke a greater opposing force. Above all, the correct timing of the aids is of paramount importance. This will improve with practice, but do remember to apply the aids as intermittent nudges. Do not clamp on the aid with increasing pressure – it won't work. Finally, be very careful to vary the number of steps requested, otherwise you teach the horse to anticipate. It is all too easy to fall into the habit of getting, say, two steps each way each time. Then, when one is asked for, or three, you will go on getting two, as before.

Jumping

So far we have done only a little mounted jumping, but it should be remembered that the loose schooling over fences will have already instilled a fairly high degree of confidence in our horse and that our work on the flat – improving physique, suppleness, balance and obedience – is in reality the best possible preparation for jumping fences successfully. Nothing is more true than the saying that if you want a horse to jump *don't* jump him. Too much jumping only sickens the horse and encourages him to seek ways of avoiding and evading. Jumping should be fun; a game, in fact, but played in accordance with rules and both horse and rider should enjoy themselves.

To vary the school work and at the same time to further the training, the horse can be ridden in the lane over the same fences that he has jumped loose, but with all of them being lowered a little. We can then put up small fences in our schooling area, expending all the ingenuity we can command to make them in as wide a variety as possible. The more coloured fences we can lay our hands on the better, within reason, but do not ignore the solid rustics.

A good exercise, if one has a suitable area, is to place six to eight, or even more, smallish fences, spreads and uprights of not more than 2 feet 6 inches, in an almost haphazard fashion round the area, jumping them as they present themselves but *never* following the same course. Jump some from trot and others from a free canter, but always return to a slower pace, i.e. trot if the fence has been jumped from canter, after clearing a fence. The fences themselves should be changed about, or altered in appearance, as frequently as possible, and it is surprising how different a fence can be made to look by the addition of plastic fertilizer sacks and the like.

Although these fences will be well within the compass of the horse, the rider should ride at them as though they were much larger and leave absolutely nothing to chance. To court a refusal by taking the horse for granted is stupid, and it is something that we never want to let enter into his head. We want our horse to know almost instinctively that, when faced with a fence, it is to be jumped.

Some people advocate a neckstrap when jumping lest the young horse should jump bigger than is expected. It is not a bad precaution to take and, if used swiftly, in an emergency it can save your horse a jab in the mouth – the surest way to stop him jumping. I prefer to do without, since the wretched thing never seems to be in the right place when I want it. If it is, then I find I tend to use it unnecessarily and find myself stiffening my position and pulling upwards. For these reasons I use a good lump of mane in an emergency, but this is only from personal experience, and others may find the neckstrap more satisfactory.

Jumping in this way once or twice a week is quite sufficient in this stage. Later we shall discuss mounted jumping in more detail.

Hacking

Although schooling has been examined in some detail and at some length in this chapter we should not forget that hacking in the open will occupy the greater part of our daily training sessions.

In the country we can increase the periods spent at a steady canter, letting the horse go on in this pace for up to one and a half miles. An occasional sharp gallop can also be introduced over a distance of up to four or five furlongs or so. The horse must not be allowed to go flat out, however, but must always gallop within himself. Logs, ditches, banks, etc., if they are not too big can be hopped over as they are found and we should make every effort to ride up and down hills as a strengthening exercise.

On the roads our horse, by now, should be virtually independent of his companion and on roads known to carry only light traffic there is no reason why he should not go out on his own. Always take the precaution, however, of riding out alone *after* the horse has done some work.

Roadwork should be carried out at a good, striding walk on a reasonable length of rein and at a slow trot. Where hills occur, the horse can be trotted up them, an exercise which makes him use himself to the full. Do, please, look where you are riding and go at a pace suitable to the conditions underfoot. Modern roads can be steeply cambered at the sides, and it is difficult for the horse to trot when this is the case. Similarly, pick your way at walk on rough, stony tracks. There is no sense in inviting trouble.

If you can find a suitable grass verge, unmarked by our small-time bureaucrats with a **No Horses** sign, make use of it. Nice rough verges, intersected with drainage grips, are very useful as a balancing exercise for both horse and rider if ridden over at either trot or canter.

If a hunting whip has not yet been carried now is the time to get the horse used to one. Failure to do so will result in your normally well-behaved horse progressing sideways like a crab when you first take him (and a hunting whip) out cubbing.

Continue, of course, to take your horse to the odd show, and if there is a suitable class enter him. Don't, however, fly too high. Show classes, if he is the right sort, won't do any harm, but keep the jumping down to the level of a Sunday afternoon club rally. It is not sensible to risk refusals for the sake of experience. At some time, at some fence, we will get a refusal and will have to deal with it accordingly, but as yet we do not want to put ourselves into the position of having to cope with one, nor is our horse ready to be put in that position, either.

Duration of Stage 3

This stage, if all goes well, may be completed in about ten weeks, taking the training up to the first weeks of September, but, of course, it all depends on the horse and whether he has so far had no ailments which would put him off work. It could extend well into September and even a few weeks beyond the end of that month.

As far as possible the horse during this period should be given his hour of freedom at grass. His feeding is necessarily according to his individual needs and the amount of work he is doing and the bulk feed throughout will consist of hay, which can be reduced in relation to his intake of grass. Otherwise he will need three feeds a day, at least, with an energy ration comprising nuts and oats of not less than 9 lb, to which bran, carrots, apples, etc., must be added. A bran or linseed mash should be given at least once a week mixed with a goodish handful of Epsom salts. Additives, such as molasses, honey, etc., or any particular supplement favoured, can also be given.

Roughly speaking, the work and exercise will remain the same but the schoolwork, interspersed with loose schooling and jumping sessions may be increased up to forty minutes daily, the lungeing sessions being about twenty minutes or so and the hacking up to one and a half hours.

As before, frequent rest periods are necessary during schooling work and, of course, daily inspections must be made to ensure that the horse is sound. If the youngster seems to be getting stale in his work and is generally dull then do not hesitate to cut the work down, or even cut it out altogether and give him a rest for a few days in his paddock, bringing him in at night.

The more time that can be devoted to systematic grooming and strapping the fitter your horse (and you) will be.

Chapter 16   Phase 2: Stage 4

This stage and the one that follows merge together to complete Phase 2 and the basic training progression with which we are concerned.

Much of the ridden schooling in this phase is concerned with the canter, for which our horse is now prepared by being in better balance and by our being able to correct his position and control his quarters with our legs. Whilst what follows is confined almost entirely to the canter, we must, of course, continue our exercises at walk and trot and also work on the turns.

From here, the lunge work decreases in importance, and though we shall use it initially to prepare for the ridden canter schooling, its use in the future will be infrequent. We may, of course, return to it for some specific purpose and may continue to use it as a means of calming the horse preparatory to riding him.

The lunge work in this stage is therefore specifically directed at the canter pace and involves short periods of cantering on the circle to either hand, with the diameter of the latter being increased and decreased with the horse remaining in balance. We may also, on the lunge, accustom him to the business of extending and shortening his stride. To start with, the extension is obtained by allowing the horse to canter on an almost straight line involving movement on the part of the trainer. Shortening takes place as the circle is resumed and will be assisted if the rein is operated in little jerks to bring the head inwards. These must be given tactfully, however, otherwise the quarters will swing out and the bend will be spoilt. Finally the circle can be maintained and the horse asked to extend a little on the larger circles and to shorten as the diameter is decreased.

To commence, lunge from the cavesson with the side-reins at cantering length, and when the work is established complete the exercise using the first method of lungeing from the bit, unless it is necessary to employ one of the other two corrective methods.

When we have got the horse cantering in-hand from the bit in both directions, and doing so fluently, we can begin the ridden exercises at the same gait.

Begin by asking for the strike-offs using lateral aids. If any difficulty is experienced, approach the corner in rising trot on the outside diagonal, acting strongly with the legs.

As the strike-offs become more easily accomplished we can, gradually, begin to effect the change-over to diagonal aids and obtain, as a result, a more balanced depart from trot into canter. The diagonal aids for the canter on the left rein are as follows. Sit in the saddle for the few strides preceding the strike-off point with the body erect but not stiff, then move your weight very slightly to the rear and on to your outside seatbone so that the forehand is lightened. Raise the left hand slightly (it raises the head and therefore lightens the shoulders) and *squeeze*, don't pull, the rein (as though you had a rubber ball in your hand). The left leg acts on the girth, the right leg behind the girth maintains the position and nudges the horse into the strike-off.

The transition will not be made smoothly, if at all, unless the hand yields at the moment the horse yields his jaw and the body remains in its upright position. If the hand fails to yield quickly enough the first stride of the leading leg is shortened and the freedom of the shoulder restricted. Should the body incline forward (a common failing), the rider peering downwards to see whether his horse is, in fact, cantering (or, perhaps it is to assure himself that the horse's leg is still in situ), the forehand will be overweighted and the horse either prevented from striking off at all or at least prevented from doing so smoothly.

Once the horse is in canter, the rider must maintain the pace by continuing to give the canter aids in time with the movement. He is, in fact, keeping the horse in the canter position all the way round the school without loss of impulsion. The movement of the rider's body at canter need be no more than a following of the movement through the undulation of the waist.

For some reason the canter strike-off, particularly in a dressage test, is a source of near-terror to many riders and they try so hard that they usually make a mess of it. In general, apart from the tenseness and over-anxious frame of mind, the fault lies in hurrying. As a result the horse is pushed off-balance. For heaven's sake, take your time and relax. If a mistake is made and the horse leads with the wrong (outside) foreleg then bring him quietly back to trot and try again. Whatever you do don't try to 'throw' him on to the correct leg by a violent movement of the body made whilst being perched over the shoulder.

The canter, of course, is a most useful – if not *the* most useful – pace for improving the longitudinal suppleness of the horse through extension and shortening of the outline.

Initially, control at canter, producing either a shortening of the posture or otherwise, can be made by manipulating the reins. If, for instance, we want the horse to extend himself we can use the outside rein to turn his nose slightly to the outside, which will give greater freedom to the inside shoulder and allow the stride of the inside foreleg to be lengthened. To shorten, we act with the inside hand, bending the head towards the leading foreleg just before it comes to the ground. Consequently, the freedom of the shoulder is restricted and the stride must shorten. This very useful technique can be used to good effect when jumping a course of obstacles, some of which will need to be jumped from a long stride (staircase, fences, etc.) and others which will require jumping from a short, bouncing stride, such as uprights. The rein action will be made more effective if the rider sits even more upright when shortening, and inclines his body slightly forward when he wants to lengthen the stride.

Shortening the stride causes a re-imposition of balance and a check in impulsion by the weight moving towards the quarters. A more sophisticated method of achieving the same object can be made by the *half-halt*, which may, of course, be used in making any downward transition or to check impulsion within the other paces. Its effectiveness is, however, very much exemplified in canter, and it is a most useful balancing exercise which has a very practical application to control in the approach to a fence. The half-halt means exactly that – it is a check causing the weight to be taken on the quarters and therefore off the forehand and is immediately followed by forward movement.

To be executed correctly, or at all, the horse must be in a state of impulsion, otherwise there is nothing to check. To make the half-halt both legs are applied briefly and decisively to send the horse further on to his bit. Almost simultaneously both hands are raised and turned upwards with the palm on top. In both cases the action is no more than momentary.

The young horse should experience no trouble in making his halts correctly at this stage and he should fall naturally into a halt, standing square with fore- and hindlegs together. Usually, the forelegs come into line easily enough, the fault, more frequently, being found in the hindlegs, one of which may tend to be carried behind the other. If this is the case, we can revert to the little trick we used much earlier on and make our halt on an element of a circle. By doing so, the inside hindleg will be brought further under the body and the position corrected. If, therefore, it is the left hindleg which is left behind at halt we will need to practise on a left-handed circle – if it is the right leg, then we must ride on a circle to the right.

38 A correct balanced halt

This 'school' halt stops the horse in a state of balance and allows the move-offs to be correspondingly balanced. Naturally, this is the position when executing a halt during a dressage test. In the show-ring, however, particularly when the horse is stood out without his saddle for inspection by the judge it is better to stand the horse with his legs, both fore and hind, about 12–18 inches apart. It makes a better impression on the eye and the horse appears to stand over a lot of ground as a result of the base being lengthened rather than shortened, as is the case when he stands at the school halt. The same convention holds good for the equestrian photograph, and it has to be admitted that the result is more pleasing, and flattering, too. But it is, of course, a little frustrating, for both horse and rider if they have perfected a school halt and cannot, understandably, get out of the habit.

As a further balancing exercise we should practise the transitions which are, also, a salutary method of bringing an over-exuberant horse to hand.

With the canter departs, on either leg, firmly established, we can begin cantering complete circles. Do not, however, overdo this exercise, nor make the circles too small, as it imposes a very considerable physical effort on the horse.

39 A free balanced canter

40 The gallop, but in balance and
under control

Jumping

The jumping training can now be advanced a step or two, whilst bearing in mind that too much jumping is the surest way to stop the horse going freely and enjoying himself over fences. It is not, therefore, necessary to jump more than once or twice a week, but towards the end of the period we can include rather more difficult fences and one largeish fence to be jumped just once during the week.

When the horse is jumping loose (which still remains as the basis for jumping), we can now, whilst at first keeping the fences low, remove the ground pole which so far we have been placing in front of the fence to help the horse judge his take-offs. It has served its purpose. By removing the pole we make the horse judge his approach and leap by looking at the *top* of the fence instead of at its base. Over low fences it makes very little difference whether the take-off is estimated by the top or the bottom, but the horse must be trained to estimate the height he has to clear when fences get bigger. To do so he must look at the top rail. When he has learnt to do without the ground pole we can begin to introduce combinations by placing our fences to give either one, two or three non-jumping strides between the obstacles.

In jumping, it can be taken that fences are *related* when they are placed between 39 feet 4 inches and 80 feet apart. Below 39 feet they become *combinations*. Between two vertical fences 24 feet from inside to inside of each fence the length allows for one non-jumping stride; 33 feet for two non-jumping strides. In the case of a vertical to a spread fence these distances are shortened by between 6 and 12 inches according to the length of stride taken by the individual horse and the speed at which the approach is made. If the combination is that of a spread fence followed by a vertical one, up to 12 inches must be added to the length between the two obstacles. In general terms, we can take 11 feet as being a good average stride at canter and allow 12 feet for the leap itself from take-off to landing. Other distances would be 45 feet for three non-jumping strides between fences, 56 feet for four non-jumping strides and 67 feet for five.

In international class jumping competitions, problems for horses and riders may be set by the course-builder increasing the distance between fences sited as combinations by about 2–3 feet. This will involve half-strides being made and the horse being therefore compelled to cope with the awkward distance by either lengthening or shortening his stride. As an example, if the distance between two fences was 48 feet the number of non-jumping strides would be three and a half, and would have to be taken as in three longer non-jumping canter strides or four shortened ones. Such problems, however, are not within the province of the young horse, and the greatest attention should be given to placing combinations at exactly the right distances so that no half-strides are introduced. Watch your horse very carefully when schooling him loose over combinations and if the distances seem to cause him any difficulty, alter them accordingly.

Incidentally, when you have got the distance right, spare a moment to observe how the horse uses his body over a fence. You will see how the extension of head and neck, and the use he makes of them in the approach and during the leap itself, contributes to the 'bascule'. The lesson to be learnt is that the rider should do nothing to interfere with these movements, and that involves the hand *following* the horse's mouth throughout and the body being so positioned as to allow the desirable arc to be formed by the horse's back over the summit of the fence.

Get the horse to jump combinations loose and also one or two fairly big fences, as much as 4 feet high. If you are quite certain that he is able to go at least 6 inches higher than that, then ride him, in the lane, over these same fences but with the top rail 6 inches lower.

41 The 'farmyard' – an excellent schooling facility at the Porlock Vale School

In the jumping area, continue to ride over a variety of small fences but also introduce one or two larger ones which can be jumped once a week. To help the horse and, incidentally, to assist you to 'see' the stride, put a placing fence, a cavalletto, two non-jumping strides in front of these fences, i.e. 33 feet. Make all the fences as wide as possible and gradually reduce your reliance on the wings. If you have no properly-constructed wings, use a standard or something similar and place a pole from that to the standard supporting the fence, placing it a good 12 inches higher than the height of the fence.

Naturally, the horse will be discouraged by these wings from running out, once he is within their enclosing influence, and will jump the lower fence as the lesser of the two evils. But wings are only there as a precaution during the early days, and as soon as possible we should begin by gradual stages to dispose of them all together.

Two further jumping exercises can be done in this stage, both commencing with a single cavalletto. The first of these is designed to discourage any tendency to rush and to encourage the horse to jump as calmly as he performs his work on the flat. Calm, incidentally, is a state of mind, and it is not synonymous with lethargy. Our horse can still be calm yet move and jump with the greatest impulsion and fire.

Place the cavalletto in the centre of the schooling area at its top height; approach from trot, jump the obstacle, and come immediately to halt. The halt is made, not by hauling the reins, but by a stretched back and a slight inclination of the shoulders to the rear as the horse touches down. To do this exercise there is no need for the rider to do more than incline his body forward as the horse takes off. If an exaggerated movement is made and the rider's seat is way out of the saddle when landing he will not be in a position to bring the horse to halt. In fact, he will be encouraging him, positively, to canter on.

When he can jump the cavelletto from both directions at trot place another cavalletto on top to make a small fence and repeat the exercise at canter. As a variation, make a square of four cavalletti the length and breadth being 33 feet, which would be two non-jumping strides if we were going to jump in and out.

42 An excellent jump over a good sort of obstacle for a young horse

Approach the square at trot, jump and halt; then jump out again, first over the cavalletto immediately in front and later over one or other of the cavalletti forming the sides of the box, which will involve a left or right turn. The second exercise encourages confidence, obedience and initiative in the horse and will stand us in good stead should we wish to go in for jumping seriously later on. It involves jumping from an angle and commences as before with a single cavalletto placed in the centre of the arena. Circle the arena at trot and then make the turn towards the obstacle – correctly please – at the centre marker on the short side. Jump the obstacle from trot and continue on the centre line, turning to the left or right as you wish when you reach the end of the manege. Carry this out a number of times, from both directions, before delaying your turn at the centre marker so that your approach, instead of being straight to the fence, is made at an angle to it. Delay making the turn by degrees until you are riding a figure-8, jumping the cavalletto at the centre of the figure from each direction. Now, add another cavalletto to make a low spread fence and go through the whole progression again at canter, until once more you are riding a figure-8, changing the leading leg at each end of the manege by coming back to trot for four or five steps before striking off on the opposite leg.

As follow-up exercises to these two the box, or square, can

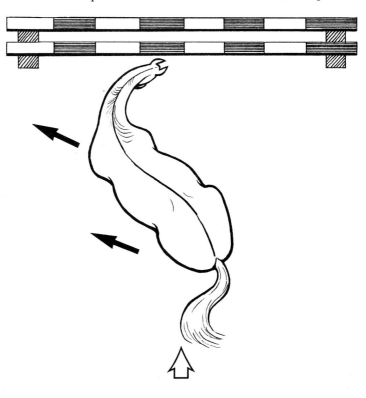

Figure 32a
The horse refuses by running out to the left.

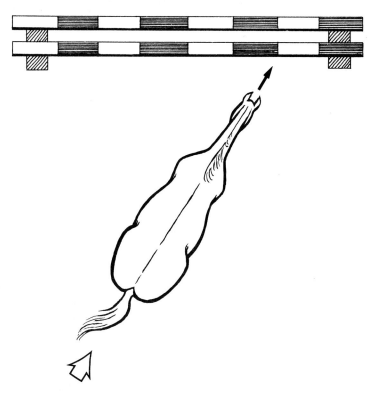

Figure 32b
The run-out to the left is corrected by jumping at an angle.

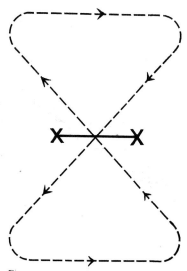

Figure 33
An exercise used to teach horse and rider to jump at an angle to the fence, in this instance a single cavalletto.

be used to jump the horse in and out at an angle. If you have sufficient space it is quite easy to work out how the four cavalletti forming the box can be jumped in a variety of patterns.

The final exercise is a little more difficult and the horse needs to be both supple and obedient and the rider fairly skilful. It involves changing direction whilst over the fence, a technique which is invaluable in jumping competitions.

Put up a small fence and, having jumped it from a straight approach, jump it at a slight angle at canter. In nine cases out of ten the horse will land, since he is on an element of a circle, as it were, with the correct foreleg leading. That is, if the fence is jumped slightly from the left he will be on a circle to the right and will land with his right foreleg leading. We can accentuate this bend to the right by inclining the horse's head in that direction whilst he is in the air or otherwise (except that we cannot stretch our backs upwards) by applying the aids for canter right. Eventually, we shall be able to jump the fence from a straight approach and bend the horse to either left or right over the obstacle, according to the disposition of the next fence.

Since in a competition there is never time for the rider to be thinking about telling his horse to change the lead, a lot must be left to the horse, who, if he is trained in this fashion, will

43 A bank, a common cross-country obstacle which in this case is being negotiated calmly and safely

come to change his leg automatically according to the altered direction asked for by his rider.

This is an appropriate point at which to consider the reasons for refusals and how they are brought about.

44 A small schooling fence

Why do Horses Refuse?

They do so for one or more of the following reasons:

1   They are over-faced, either by the fence being just too high or because they lack experience.

2   They may be sore from having jarred their legs or from a strained back.

3   They will stop if they believe that the act of jumping will result in pain. An ill-fitting saddle too low at the wither, which pinches the back when it is rounded over the fence is a sure way to stop a horse jumping. Even more sure is the jab in the mouth received from an incompetent rider. Indeed, even the memory of pain may cause a horse to refuse long after the source of the pain has been removed. The horse who was once jumped when his shins were sore may not recover his confidence until long after the trouble has cleared up. Such reasons may, in fact, account for the sudden inexplicable stop made by the normally reliable horse. Certainly, if a horse has had a bad experience at a particular type of fence it will take a lot of patient work before he jumps the same fence with confidence again.

4   They will stop under an incompetent or nervous rider. It is of no use at all attempting to teach a young horse to jump unless you are quite confident about the business yourself and have learnt the job on older, experienced jumpers.

Indecision and nervousness in the rider apart, there are certain elementary faults committed by the inexperienced rider which, on a young horse particularly, contribute towards making him disobedient at fences. Young horses have not had time to acquire the steadiness of their elders and occasionally like all young things they will be a little naughty. The object uppermost in the rider's mind, therefore, should be never to give the opportunity to the horse to disobey in front of fences. To do so requires a strong but infinitely gentle rider.

I think the principal fault today is for riders to be so indoctrinated with the idea of not being left behind that other aspects suffer as a result. Of course, the rider must not be left behind, but carrying the practice of getting forward beyond reasonable limits is almost as heinous a crime. The rider is in a position of the greatest control and security when he 'follows' the movement of his horse. He loses control, and in the approach the drive of his back and seat, when he 'leads' the movement over the fence. If this sounds like splitting hairs, let me illustrate the point further.

Possibly to avoid getting left behind, the novice rider gets into his 'jumping position' well before the approach to the fence, perching on his fork with seatbones rather out of the saddle. He then uses his legs, as best he can, and increases the speed as he goes into the fence. As he does so, his hands creep forward in anticipation of the leap. In consequence, the horse through going faster is not either in a state of impulsion or balance. He stretches out his neck and has his weight on his forehand as he gets into the take-off zone, and by this time contact with his mouth has been lost. The old-stager will steady himself, raise his head of his own accord and get over – but not so the young horse. He has been put in a position in which the easiest thing for him to do is to either stop or duck out sideways. The rider has, in fact, created a situation in which it is easier for the horse to disobey than to jump.

On a young horse, and for any horse, approach the jump steadily, shoulders held straight and back inclined slightly forward, with the seat firmly in the saddle and the horse well on the hand. Make a slight check, scarcely noticeable when done correctly, by means of a quick half-halt if necessary, so as to get your horse balanced, and push on in the last three strides with the squeeze given by the legs increasing in intensity up to the final one which tells him to take off. Follow the head, but resist the impulse to drop the hands entirely – on take-off the horse, after stretching his head and neck, raises them and lifts his forehead preparatory to pushing off with his hindlegs. At this point lead your own movement forward with your *shoulders* not by shooting your hands forward, which would result in your being left behind. Your object in the flight phase of the jump is to have your spine in line with that of the horse and that won't happen if you jump the fence before he does. Let your horse jump 'in front' of *you* don't jump in front of *him*.

As a colleague of mine once wrote about jumping, 'sit on your bum and steer for the guns'. Elsewhere in his piece he described 'the protuberance at the end of my back' as 'the jewel in the horseman's crown'. He wasn't far wrong either.

5 Finally, horses can refuse, with justification, if they find themselves completely wrong at a fence. They show their good sense by doing so and should not be punished.

How do Horses Refuse?

Very simply they either put the brakes on and stop, or they duck out sideways and run out.

In the first case, if they stop for none of the reasons given previously, they do so because they have not been made sufficiently obedient to the leg – they have not learnt to **Go Forward**.

Similarly, if they run out for none of the reasons given, the rider has not acquired sufficient control over the quarters, which initiate the run-out by making a change of direction.

In theory, if we are horsemasters, trainers and riders of an infallibility unlikely to be encountered amongst flesh and blood mortals, our horses should never refuse a fence. In practice, it will happen to the best of us.

In training, should the horse run out, circle him quickly but quietly and have your assistant (it's always a good idea to have one handy) lower the fence immediately. Turn the horse off the circle and present him at the fence at a slight angle from the side to which he ran out. That is, if he went out to the left bring him in from the left, which will make it virtually impossible for him to run out to the same side again. Be careful, however, not to come in at too shallow an angle; otherwise you will be asking the horse to run out across the front of the fence to the right. Jump the fence two or three times again and so on for a couple of days thereafter before putting it back to its original height. Just be sure, of course, that it wasn't impossibly high at the start. Deal with a stop in the same way without employing the angled approach technique and be sure to drive on firmly with the seat. A common mistake following a stop is to make too much of a thing of the subsequent attempt. Don't waste any time and give the horse time to think, but instead circle him, using your aids fairly strongly and bring him in to the fence again, after it has been lowered, off the circle. Give the horse the benefit of the doubt always, and only when he refuses the lowered fence and you are quite sure that this is a display of naughtiness should he get one good slap across the bottom to remind him of the rules of the game.

It is not very sensible, incidentally, to go through the strange ritual of 'showing' the horse the fence. Fences, after all, are not built to be looked at but to be jumped.

When a horse is taken up to a fence, patted and then *turned away* from it, possibly with yet another pat and much cooing of 'good boy' and the like, is it surprising that when presented at it he runs out? The rider has told him what to do and rewarded him for it only a moment before. How was he to know that this time he was supposed to jump the thing!

Hacking

Hacking continues on much the same lines as before but on the roads we should be able to ride unaccompanied. On suitable going we can work up to a sustained steady canter of up to two or more miles, provided the horse is fit and clear in his wind.

On quiet lanes and bridlepaths we can add another small item to our school lessons by teaching the horse to move diagonally across from one side to the other. It will give him a little idea of the lateral work which will follow, and is in any case a useful accomplishment.

To execute the manoeuvre from left to right, apply the right rein intermittently to bend the head slightly to the right and give the wither little shoves with your left hand. At the same time weight your right seatbone, keep your right leg going on the girth and apply your left leg slightly behind the girth from front to rear. In a surprisingly short space of time the horse will move diagonally across the road and may even cross his legs for one or two strides.

This and the following stage will occupy the time up to and beyond the end of the progression with which we are concerned; until December, in fact.

During this stage, cub-hunting will have certainly commenced and we may take our horse out to see hounds on a few occasions. This aspect of the training, however, will be dealt with in the next chapter under a separate heading.

As our horse is stabled (or virtually so, since the odd hour he has been allowed at grass is of no consequence), no new routine is made necessary by the onset of the Autumn and its inevitable follower, Winter.

To keep his coat clean the horse should have been wearing a light sheet when stabled and so the fitting of rugs, etc., are not likely to be a problem.

However, he will need to be **Clipped** out, and whilst there is no reason to think that he will object, it is as well to exercise foresight in the planning of the operation.

First, of course, check that the clipping machine is in good working order and is fitted with a new set of blades. Faulty machines and blunt blades that pull the hair are one of the prime reasons for horses who are troublesome to clip. Secondly, make sure that the box you intend using is well lit. You cannot do your work in the dark, and an electric light is not much help because of the shadows it casts.

For two or three days before clipping is planned take the machine into the horse's box and get him used to your rubbing all over with it, including his head, without the engine being switched on. Make quite a business of this, passing the machine between the fore- and hindlegs and along the underside of the belly. Then switch the machine on for some minutes at a time, preferably whilst he is at his haynet, or is being attended to in some way. Carry out this little precautionary gambit three or four times during the day until he takes no notice of the noise. Finally, with the engine running, pass the machine over his body, starting on the shoulder, which is the least sensitive part, but keep the blades raised and make no attempt to cut the hair. Usually, the horse will make no objection, even when the machine is placed gently on his nose. Many, in fact, appear to enjoy the warm sensation it gives.

All this may seem to be a lot of mountain-making out of mole-hills, but for the trivial effort expended it is worthwhile doing everything possible to ensure a trouble-free session on the day.

Give the horse his usual exercise the day before clipping and work him quietly the next morning before giving him his feed. His coat should be clean enough as he has been groomed and strapped thoroughly, but give him an extra good brushing before starting to clip. Allow him a few moments to get used to the machine again and give him a haynet to keep him occupied. Then, starting on the shoulder, begin to clip. The quicker one works, within reason, the better, since boredom, resulting in an attack of the fidgets, is as much an enemy to clipping as anything else. There is really no reason why our horse, who is so used to us and to submitting to all the strange things we ask of him, should be frightened since we have never (or should have never) given him any reason to fear us. If he does get nervous, however, we must take time off to reassure him, and it will not be time wasted since a frightened horse can well begin to sweat, and when that happens no blades will be able to cope.

Although our horse trusts us and we him it is better not to

tempt providence, and to have an assistant to hold up a fore-leg whilst we deal with the awkward and ticklish parts and whilst we are working round the rear. Familiarity is all very well, but even with the quietest horse it is better to take sensible precautions and not to presume upon his good nature.

The head, understandably from the horse's viewpoint, is the most difficult and tricky part, and it is probably best to give the horse a break, letting him eat his lunch in comfort, before tackling it.

For the most part, well-brought up horses will suffer you to clip out their heads and clean the hair from their ears with no more than a few tremors and an occasional toss when the vibration becomes too much. Appreciating that the horse's head, where the bones are so near the surface, is really rather like a sound box, we must recognize that a clipping machine is not entirely pleasant. Be careful, then, not to bang bony protuberances. But, whilst being careful, get the job over as quickly as is reasonably possible.

There are a few horses who just will not keep still when their heads are being clipped and finish up by becoming a danger to themselves and to their handlers. I am absolutely against the use of a twitch, and would do everything possible and impossible to avoid employing one. On the other hand, I admit that five minutes' discomfort, in which the job is completed, is better than a couple of hours' battle in which both parties will be in danger of losing their tempers and in which either might get hurt.

A twitch, by the way, is a stout length of wood about 18 inches long with a hole bored at one end through which a loop of binder twine or something similar is passed. The loop is put round the upper lip of the horse and tightened (not too much, please) by twisting the stick. It's rather like applying a tourniquet. The effect is to cause the animal such discomfort that he is more concerned with what is happening to his nose than to what the clipper is doing. Since the twitch stops the circulation you will need to massage the horse's nose when the twine is loosened and removed.

This is one type of twitch, but there are others operating on the mouth which I understand are just as effective and are claimed, by many authorities, to be more humane. The simplest of these is a piece of soft rawhide which is placed in the mouth and over the poll like a bridle but which can be tightened so that the leather pulls upwards in the mouth.* The most sophisticated form, acting on the same principle, is the Barnum device, which employs a soft rubber bit which can be

---

*A further variation is to pass the rawhide (or it can be a piece of soft rope) above the top incisors so that it lies on the gum beneath the upper lip. This device is known as a Cherokee twitch.

tightened up by means of an ingenious arrangement of loops and rings, in much the same way as the rawhide affair.

If you feel you must use a twitch I suggest that before you do so you should get an assistant to try holding the nose with her hand, giving a tweak as necessary – it often works. It is unforgiveable to put a twitch on a horse's ear and stupid into the bargain, since it will almost certainly make him head-shy.

If you don't like the idea of a twitch, you might get the vet to give the horse a tranquillizer (much like a dentist giving his patient a whiff of gas) or you are faced with leaving the head unclipped. And if it is, well, it isn't the end of the world is it?

Fortunately for us there are only a very few horses who will go to extreme lengths to prevent our clipping their heads. Most of them submit with reasonable grace to quiet, confident handling.

Chapter 17   Phase 2 : Stage 5

Much of the work described in the last stage is applicable to this final one, but in this a new and important element enters into the training, namely hunting.

Towards the end of September the horse can be taken to cub-hunting meets, and during the season proper a few half-days in the hunting field will be very beneficial to him.

Our pupil should by now be a useful horse, obedient to the aids, physically able to comply with our wishes and mentally, also, since his limited brain power has never been overtaxed. But he lacks experience, and there is no better place than the hunting field to acquire this essential. Hunting develops his self-reliance, his initiative and his confidence. It teaches him to look after himself in all kinds of situations.

Despite his training, hunting will cause him to become excited, and so the first few occasions on which he sees hounds he must be ridden intelligently.

Cub-hunting is the ideal introduction for the youngster as it is unlikely, at least in the early part of the season during September, that any run will ensue. The purpose of cub-hunting is to introduce the young hounds to their quarry, the fox, and to do the same thing for the fox cubs. Much of the time, therefore, is spent with hounds in covert, and galloping and jumping are reduced to a minimum – ideal conditions, in fact, for our young pupil.

On the first occasion it is better if the youngster can be accompanied by an older companion who knows the ropes. If possible, hack on to the meet, which will mean getting up early as the first cub-hunting meets start at about 7 a.m., to give the horse time to settle down and get the itch out of his heels. If boxing is made necessary by the distance involved, unload at least three or four miles from the meet and hack on from there.

At the meet let the horse see what is going on, but keep him on the move and well on the outskirts of the gathering. Don't follow hounds as they move off, but instead ride away in the opposite direction and then take a route which will bring you within sight and sound of the goings on but at a safe distance away – a field or two, in fact. Stay out for an hour or two and then hack quietly home, clean the horse and give him his breakfast.

After two or three meets you and the horse can enter a little further into the body of the kirk, but again, don't hang about, keep your horse moving quietly for most of the time. If you do get a little gallop, go along quietly, well away from the bulk of the field and avoid getting jammed up in narrow lanes. If you find something small in your way, then jump it quietly as you would at home, but don't go out of your way to find fences. You are not on your own property, and to jump without cause rightly incurs the displeasure of the Master.

Undoubtedly, your horse will be rather more on his toes than usual, and he will probably take a somewhat stronger hold of his bit, but you must do everything possible, which will include making use of your head, to keep him in an acceptable state of calm. When he is excited and behaves stupidly, curb your exasperation and draw on all your reserves of tolerance.

If the horse has behaved well and is fit there is an awful temptation to think about having a season's hunting on him. Banish the thought from your mind, and realize that he is not yet ready.

After 1 November, when the season starts, take him for the odd half-day with hounds by all means, but half-a-dozen such outings is quite enough, and after Christmas it is as well to stop and continue with the normal schooling and exercise until the end of April, when he can be given a short holiday at grass.

When hunting, jump such obstacles as you meet, providing they are within your horse's compass, but do not be too proud to turn away from the nasty place if you think it is too much for him. However good the day, go home after lunch, and resist the temptation to stay out for 'just another ten minutes'. Hack quietly back to your box so that when you reach it the horse is dry and calm; if it is wet, then trot the last half-mile, put the rug on inside-out and he will be dry, or almost so, by the time you get home.

Ridden Schooling

In this last stage the secondary education will be completed by teaching the horse to go in a plain short-cheeked double bridle, by commencing a little lateral work and by teaching the rein back, although we shall, of course, continue our other schooling exercises.

So far our horse has been ridden in a plain snaffle bridle without the addition of martingales or any other extraneous objects. Now he must be *taught* to respond to the actions of a double bridle which will allow the rider a more sophisticated contact with the mouth and will help our horse to flex his lower jaw and poll in a manner which is not entirely possible in a snaffle. These two bridles are the only ones required in the case of the properly trained horse, and if at this stage we spend hours searching through tack rooms and saddlers' shops for the 'key' to our horse's mouth then, somewhere in the progression, we have gone very wrong.

No mention has yet been made of the ubiquitous drop noseband, and readers accustomed to seeing it used on every conceivable type of equine as a matter of course may wonder at the omission.

In many ways there is nothing wrong with the drop noseband. It has, after all, been an integral part of the Continental bridle for generations. Nor do I deny that it can be useful; indeed I have written numerous articles describing its action and extolling its virtues. But I am no longer convinced that it is a necessity, and I am made increasingly aware that in many instances it encourages the very reactions which it is supposed to prevent.

If you ask a group of riders why their horses are wearing drop nosebands I will guarantee that ninety per cent will be struck dumb whilst the remaining ten per cent will burble something about 'holding him' or 'shutting the mouth'. If I sound a little too omniscient, I assure readers that I have tried the experiment on numerous occasions with this result.

Correctly adjusted, with the nosepiece about three inches above the nostrils and resting on the soft end of the nasal bone, very little restriction of the breathing occurs, but a *certain* amount of restriction, even though it may not be significant, is present. The action otherwise is aimed at lowering the horse's head so that it is placed in a position which allows the bit to act effectively on the bars and gives the rider maximum control. That is, the head is carried a little in advance of the vertical so that the bit acts across the bars. It therefore prevents our horse getting his nose into the air and so becoming above our hand and out of our control.

This object is achieved by pressure on the rein causing the horse to 'give', or to retract, slightly his lower jaw. Since, however, his jaws are encompassed by the nosepiece of the drop noseband and the rear strap fastened beneath the bit, the result of the retraction is to transmit pressure to the nose which, combined with a little check being placed on the breathing apparatus, causes the horse to lower his head. Of course, it will prevent the horse from opening his mouth and evading the action of the bit in that way. And that is an evasion with which an awful lot of people seem to be obsessed. So obsessed, indeed, are some folk about a horse opening his mouth that they slap a drop noseband on as a preventative against such a happening without, I suspect, finding out whether their horse indulges in this particular evasion or not.

Now I can see that a drop noseband may serve a useful purpose on a headstrong, impetuous horse, but the young horse has hardly had time to show his propensities or otherwise in this direction, so that is no reason for fitting the device.

On the other hand, if he does open his mouth you can certainly shut it by putting a strap round his two jaws, but you don't stop him *trying* to open it. In fact, as force provokes force, his reaction is likely to be even more violent, and the end-product of the exercise may be far worse than the first evasion. Similarly, if he doesn't open his mouth, the fitting of a drop noseband is a jolly good way of encouraging him to do so. He has been supplied with a base against which to resist. So, why fit a drop noseband on a youngster?

Let us return to the double bridle, which should comprise a light bradoon and a short-cheeked bit fitted with a curb chain. The design of bit and bradoon is largely a matter of preference, the main differences being whether the cheek of the bit is fixed, when no movement of the mouthpiece can take place, or whether it is of the sliding variety, where the cheek passes through a hole in the butt end of the mouthpiece and allows a small degree (up to perhaps half an inch) of movement in the latter.

Frequently the bradoon which accompanies the fixed cheek bit follows the same theme and is made with eggbutt cheeks, which, whilst they will not pinch the lips, will again preclude movement of the mouthpiece. The bradoon used with a slide-cheek bit is nearly always made with a loose ring, i.e. one that passes through a hole in the mouthpiece, and so movement of the latter in the mouth is made possible.

The argument in favour of the slide-cheek bit and the loose ring bradoon is that the combination allows the horse to 'mouth' his bit and keep his mouth 'wet' with the saliva produced. This is the same argument advanced for using a 'mouthing' bit fitted with keys. The argument against, and it is that advanced by the disciples of the fixed cheek principle, is that, although this may be all very well, it encourages an unsteadiness in the head, and since the mouthpiece moves there must be a greater risk of the bit acting unevenly and indefinitely. Further, a slide cheek is more severe, or capable of being more severe, because the movement of the cheek allows a little greater leverage.

Those are the arguments for and against, and all of them are tenable. It is up to you to decide which side appears to have the more logical case and to act accordingly. What do I recommend? To be honest, I prefer to use a fixed cheek curb with a light *loose ring* bradoon, and I don't think I have a logical argument to present for this compromise. I just feel that both sides have points, and so I choose a middle course. And if that isn't sitting on the fence with a vengeance, I don't know what is.

However, having chosen a bit and bradoon it is as well to understand just what they are going to do in the horse's mouth. By doing so we will appreciate how delicate and subtle an instrument is the double bridle.

The bradoon, fitted above the curb bit, acts upon the corners of the mouth to raise the head of the trained horse. The curb, when it assumes an angle of 45 degrees or more in the horse's mouth in response to rein pressure, acts upon three parts of the head, inducing it to be lowered, whilst the nose is retracted at the poll and in the lower jaw. The mouthpiece has a tongue port at its centre which encourages the tongue to be raised up into the declivity provided and, therefore, away from the bars of the mouth. The bearing surface on either side of the port then lies directly on the *bars*, the area of gum between the incisor and molar teeth. The action of the mouthpiece is downward and slightly to the rear, and is assisted by the curb chain tightening in the *curb groove* as the eye of the bit, to which it is attached, is inclined forward. The effect is to make the horse lower his head and flex his lower jaw, whilst retracting his nose. The lowering influence is assisted further by pressure being applied to the *poll*. This is made possible by the forward movement of the eye of the bit, attached to the cheek-pieces of the bridle, which transmits a downward pressure via the cheekpieces to the headpiece of the bridle.

These two bits in the horse's mouth, acting upon various parts, give us, at one and the same time, the ability to position the head by raising, lowering and bringing the nose inwards. But once again these complexities are beyond the capacity of the horse's understanding, and he must be accustomed gradually to the diverse actions of the double bridle. Failure to teach the horse the responses required of him can only result in his becoming confused and in being driven into making defensive resistances against pressures the meaning of which he does not comprehend.

We begin, therefore, at the beginning – in his stable. Fit the bridle carefully, the bradoon just wrinkling the corners of the lips, the curb bit below resting on the bars centrally, being neither so high as to come into contact with the molars nor so low as to meet the incisors. The butt ends of both curb and bradoon should project between a quarter and a half inch each side of the mouth. The eye of the bit should be bent out-wards away from the face so that it does not chafe when in use. If the eyes are not so bent the required outward inclination can be given by placing them in a vice and pulling them out. The curb chain must then be adjusted to lie flat with the fly link (that's the additional one hanging in the centre of the chain through which is passed the lipstrap) at the bottom. The curb chain should lie flush in the groove when the bit assumes its angle of 45 degrees. Too tight a curb is unkind and unnecessary, and will only cause him pain and consequently resistance, but too loose a chain is almost as bad. Fitted too loosely, the chain will rise out of the groove and chafe the virtually unprotected jawbones above.

Most people prefer a double link curb chain rather than a single-link one, but there is much to be said in favour of using a curb of soft leather or even of strong elastic. I, and many others possessed of far better hands than mine, have frequently used the latter successfully on fussy horses, and I believe that the mildness of the action encourages co-operation. In any case, I would advise that the curb chain used on a young horse should be fitted with a rubber sleeve.

Otherwise check the fitting of the browband to see that it is not too small, therefore pulling the headpiece against the ears; see that the throatlatch allows at least the width of three fingers between it and the throat, otherwise the horse is throttled when he attempts to bring his head up and inwards, and make sure that the noseband is fitted to allow for the insertion of two fingers.

Having satisfied yourself that the bridle fits *perfectly* put a feed in the manger and let the horse eat it with his bridle on. To do so, he must relax his lower jaw, which is the first lesson he has to learn. Let him eat a small feed in this way each day for three or four days. The next step is to put the bridle on in the box and place the horse's quarters into the corner so that he cannot retreat from the action of the bits. Pass the reins over the horse's head then take the bradoon rein in the left hand, holding it some ten inches from the bit rings and above the nose. Hold the bit reins in the right hand, the same distance from the bit, but behind the horse's chin. Now raise the head a few times by the bradoon rein, then bring the curb rein into play and ask the horse to drop his nose and relax his lower jaw to its action. Practise these two actions separately with the hands operating in a series of small vibrations. *Yield the moment the horse yields*, and be content with a very little at the start. If the horse resists the movement of the curb by a muscular contraction counteract it by employing the bradoon.

When the horse understands what is wanted and responds to alternate pressures of the two hands, take him into the school, positioning yourself as before with the reins held as described, and get the horse to walk forwards whilst you, of course, walk backwards. To encourage him to walk and to make very sure that he does not retreat from the trainer, the assistant can be placed behind the horse to follow him up. Let the hands be passive until the walk is established and then carry out the flexion exercises as before whilst in movement.

Finally, place the reins over the neck in their proper place and stand facing forward on the nearside with the bradoon held in the right hand and the curb in the left, both hands being, of course, behind the horse's head and held at approximately the same height as the reins would be normally. Raise the head slightly with the bradoon and then ask, by a manipulation of the fingers, for the horse to flex to the right and to the left. When he can do this at halt carry out the same exercise at walk, altering the direction according to which side you are applying the flexion. Correct any resistance and any undue lowering with the bradoon rein.

You should be able within a week or so to obtain a walk round the school to either hand with the horse flexing correctly. He will then be ready to be ridden in the double bridle, and since he has already learnt its actions and is accustomed to them neither he nor his rider should experience any untoward difficulties.

You may find, however, that to start with your legs will have to operate actively to push the horse into acceptance of the bit and it would, of course, be unwise to ask too much or to work at anything but walk for some days. Only when the horse responds to the bridle easily at walk should you school at trot, and only when he goes happily in that pace should you attempt the canter exercises.

With a thick-jowled horse, who will have difficulty in carrying his head and flexing in accordance with the more advanced requirements of the double bridle, one must go very slowly indeed, and not expect to reach the standard that will be obtained with a horse of better conformation.

In fact, there are horses who cannot accept a double bridle due to the conformation of their mouths. Usually, these are the thick-set, cobby sorts who are short and broad in the jaw. They just do not have room in their mouths for the double bridle, and it is hopeless to persist with one. Such horses are ideally suited to a Pelham. This is not a bit of which I am particularly fond but in these cases it often suits very well, although, recognizing the limitations of the horse, it will not be possible to reach anywhere near the balanced head-carriage that can be obtained with the better-bred horse.

Incidentally, if it is true that this sort of horse cannot take a double bridle it is equally true that a more breedy horse, whose jaws are narrower and longer, cannot accommodate a Pelham. In these cases the long jaw causes the mouthpiece to be placed fairly high in relation to the curb groove, with the result that the curb chain rises, inevitably, out of the groove to act upon the jaw bones when the curb rein of the Pelham is operated.

The **Rein-Back**, or the teaching of it, is delayed to this late stage for a very good reason, which is that until the horse is in the correct form with a good engagement of the hocks and until he has acquired free forward movement, any attempt to rein-back, or to do so correctly, is doomed to failure. Indeed, the rein-back is not a movement which is easy to execute correctly and certainly not before the horse is confirmed in going forward.

No one could be a greater admirer of the Pony Club and all its works than myself, but on one point, the rein-back, I disagree with it profoundly. Very frequently it is asked of small children on wholly unschooled ponies, and I have even seen children *rein-backing* through a lane made with a couple of straw bales on each side. That is asking for something like eight paces to the rear, which is something not asked for even in Grand Prix dressage. As a result, there is a very prevalent idea that one must lean back and pull in order to make the horse go backwards. I have even heard an instructor advising her pupils to *lean back*. That, of course, has nothing to do with the *rein-back* proper, and the time spent on hauling backwards through straw bales would be put to better use by teaching horses and ponies to go forward – which is far more important since no horse can go backwards (under control that is) until he has first learnt to go forward.

As with many other movements, we commence by putting the idea into the horse's head from the ground. You will remember that very early in the training we caused the horse to move back in the stable, and we should have continued these little stable lessons right up to this point. If we have done so, we can take the horse into the school and walk him down the side. The horse is then slowed down and brought to a balanced halt when the trainer alters his position so that he stands directly in front of the horse. Holding the reins in either hand he causes the horse to lower his head. He then acts *alternately* with each rein, and, if this does not produce a pace to the rear, treads on the horse's toes.

The rein-back is **not** a walk backwards, since the walk is a pace of four-time and the rein-back is one of two-time employing the legs in diagonal pairs. The pace to the rear which is taken, therefore, must be made with a diagonal pair moving to the rear in unison. Two paces are sufficient, and the horse should then be urged forward smartly. Above all, he should be given no encouragement to turn the rein-back into a run-back.

To carry out the exercise mounted, when the horse moves back in-hand quite straight and without swinging the quarters, use the wall again, since this will prevent a swing in that direction. Ride actively into halt and almost immediately ask for the rein-back by acting with the hands and releasing the legs whilst keeping them in light contact. The hands, once more, act alternately, and, if used tactfully, the signal of the right hand will result in the horse taking a pace to the rear with the right diagonal, i.e. right foreleg and left hind. Conversely, the use of the left hand activates the left diagonal. Having obtained one step, pause for a fraction of a second before asking for the second one so that each step is clearly defined. Just as important is the disposition of the rider's weight. It will be obvious that any shift to the rear of the rider's body will act to overweight the quarters, limiting their movement and causing the horse, most probably, to place his hindleg out sideways in a natural opposition instead of directly to the rear. The rider must therefore free the quarters by lightening his seat, which is easiest done by pressing down on both irons.

A point to remember about the action of the hands and a common fault is for the arms to 'give' whilst the hands are 'taking', which makes the action an entirely negative one. The resistance must come from the shoulders, and this is true of all such rein actions.

Finally, having obtained two clear steps backwards, ride **Forward** immediately. Later on you may work up to as many as four steps, but two is enough for now.

To reiterate, do not attempt the rein-back until

a You have free forward movement,

b Until you have so suppled and strengthened the hindlegs that they are able to give you a square halt. If the horse cannot halt squarely he cannot rein-back either.

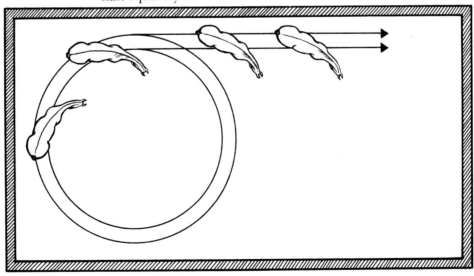

Figure 34
Right Shoulder-in
made from a
circle.

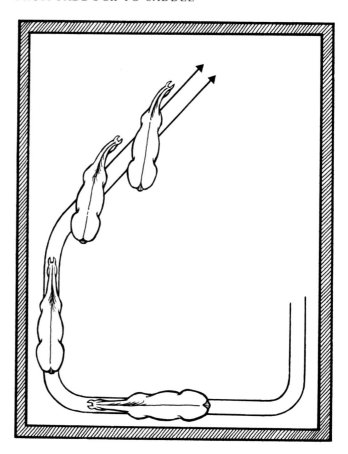

Figure 35
Stages in half-pass to the right.

Work on Two Tracks

Two-track work, where the fore- and hindlegs follow different tracks, begins with the exercise known as 'Shoulder-in', and has its aim in the performance of the 'Half-Pass'. But at its root is the work done on the circle, with the horse bent correctly in the direction of the movement, and, also in the half-turns on forehand and haunches which involved crossing the legs, a prerequisite of the work on two tracks and which gave us control over the quarters. Until the horse can perform these movements, lateral work, or work on two tracks, is out of the question. Indeed, if we think about it, the riding of the circle in the correct bend is the foundation of all movements and of all control.

In shoulder-in the horse is bent from poll to tail with his head *away* from the direction of the movement. He travels sideways, but always moving forward in the direction of his convex side. The legs of the opposite concave side pass in front and cross over those of the convex side.

In half-pass, when the horse ultimately moves diagonally across the school, the horse is straight, or virtually so, only his

45 The first strides of half-pass to the right

head being slightly towards the direction in which he is travelling. Again, the legs must cross over, the outside legs (left in the half-pass to the right) passing over the inside ones.

To perform shoulder-in, and ultimately the half-pass, we must understand the workings of the more advanced rein aids, the fourth, the *indirect rein of opposition in front of the withers*, and particularly the fifth, *the indirect rein of opposition behind the withers*, sometimes called the *intermediary rein*.

In the first instance, taking the right rein as an example, the hand acts strongly in front of the withers in the direction of the left shoulder. The left rein first yields and then supports in a direction parallel to the horse's spine. Both legs act equally to maintain impulsion. The result is that the nose is turned a little to the right, which causes the weight to fall on the left shoulder. Thus the forehand is compelled to move to the left in order for the horse to remain in balance. The fifth rein, behind the withers, has the effect of moving the whole horse sideways.

In the instance of the right rein the hand acts behind the withers, without crossing them, in the direction of the left hip. The left rein yields, then supports parallel to the neck. Both legs act to maintain impulsion whilst the weight is put first on the right seatbone to get the movement started and then on to the left once it is under way. The horse moves forward and to the left on parallel tracks crossing his right legs over his left. This last is the rein with which we shall clearly be most concerned in lateral work.

Shoulder-in, although it sounds rather mystifying, is, in fact, nothing more than a supreme suppling exercise, improving the balance and preparing the horse for oblique travel. It is most easily obtained from the circle, when the horse is already prepared by being bent in the direction of the movement. Therefore, we commence by riding a fairly large circle, let us say a left-handed one which will lead us to left shoulder-in. Continue to circle until you have obtained exactly the right bend, then execute, as you come to the wall, a few steps of shoulder-in by applying the following aids. Holding the bend we apply the left *indirect rein of opposition behind the withers* (*the intermediary rein*) just as the forelegs are leaving the track along the wall and whilst the hindlegs are still on it. The right hand, after yielding, supports in line with the neck. The right leg, slightly behind the girth, controls any exaggerated swing of the quarters to the right whilst the left leg acts on the girth to maintain the impulsion and also to reinforce the action of the left rein, which, by opposing, is driving the quarters to the right. Having the horse correctly bent for the circle, after a few steps we can push him forward again and ride a circle once more.

46 Just entering shoulder-in from
the circle

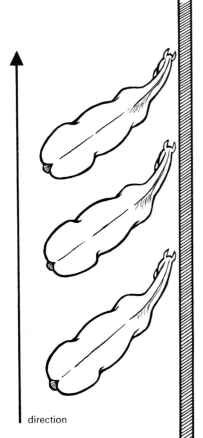

direction

Figure 36a
The exercise known as 'head-to-
the-wall' (travers), which is
approached again from the circle.

To attempt shoulder-in from a straight line is almost impossible with a young horse, for it entails putting him into the
correct bend in the space of a second and then, of course,
having to return to a straight line and start the process all over
again. In riding the exercise from a circle and then returning
to the same figure the bend remains constant. It will be seen
that half-pass can be taught directly from shoulder-in, but,
frankly, it is difficult to execute correctly, and the movement
is probably best approached from the *Head to the Wall* exercise
(also and possibly, confusingly, known as *quarters-in* or *travers*).

It is, however, easier to return to our half-volte, which we used when leading up to the half-turn on the quarters, and to ride that figure with quarters-in returning to the track by a few steps at half-pass. Here we shall, in fact, be promoting forward movement instead of slowing it down, which is a tendency apparent in the conventional head-to-tail exercise leading to the half-pass.

As we begin the return to the track the aids for half-pass to the left are: right *indirect rein* (on the neck) with right leg held slightly to the rear, so as to drive the shoulders to the left; the left rein then inclines the head to the left whilst the left leg acts to maintain the impulsion; the left seatbone is weighted.

Once we can obtain half-pass in this manner we can move on to obtaining it on a straight line by practising the conventional head-to-wall exercise, moving the horse obliquely first at a shallow angle of no more than 25–30 degrees and later increasing it to 45 degrees. Head to the wall can then be followed by tail to the wall (*renvers*), i.e. opposite way round, so that the wall can no longer act as a guide.

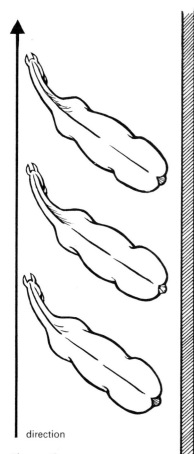

direction

Figure 36b
'Tail-to-the-wall' (renvers).

Figure 37
Approaching half-pass from lateral march. The centre figure shows the intermediate position with the horse almost straight but still moving laterally. The final (right-hand) position shows the horse flexed in the direction of the movement and in half-pass.

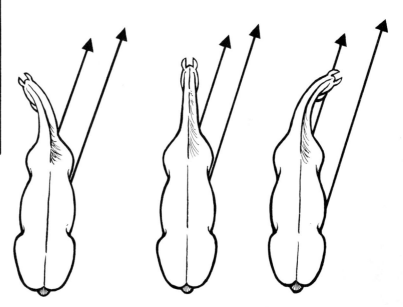

Still later we can perform the half-pass at the diagonal, which is vastly more difficult since the quarters can quite easily lead the movement instead of the head. In addition it is here that the horse anticipates to a greater degree than elsewhere. To avoid this latter, never execute the same number of steps in succession. We can begin the diagonal half-pass as we leave a corner, make a few steps, then walk straight on for a few more steps, and then go into half-pass again, and so on.

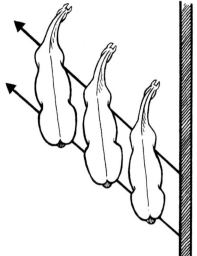

Figure 38
Lateral march to the left. The correct position is for the shoulders slightly to precede the quarters.

The final work at half-pass involves the counter changes of hand. They sound terrifying but, in fact, consist of nothing more than half-passing to the left (or right) and then doing the same thing in the opposite direction without making a break.

The horse is straightened during the last step of half-pass and is then put into the first step in the opposite direction by a reversal of the aids, the shoulders leading the movement. Opinions will vary greatly on how the half-pass should be reached, but the method described is probably as easy as any. Some authorities, however, prescribe teaching half-pass from the movement lateral march, as in Figure 39.

Lateral march to the right is obtained by the left *intermediary* rein, with the left leg acting and right supporting, and weight held on the right seatbone. There is then a transitional period in which the head is brought to the right and the right leg begins to act on the girth, whilst the left supports. On some horses this will be found to have better results, and it is mentioned because it is always as well to have an extra trick at one's disposal.

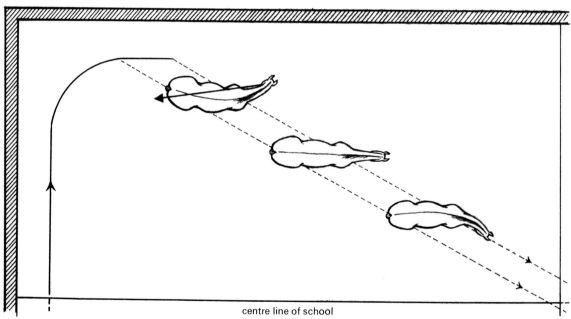

centre line of school

Figure 39
A further diagram showing half-pass to the right obtained from lateral march. The initial rein aid is the indirect rein of opposition behind the withers.

47 A schooled horse under an educated rider is so obedient that he can be ridden safely without a bit

Index